"Can I Sack The B*****d?"

A Practical Guide To Discipline And Dismissal

Kate Russell

Edited by Derek Eccleston

RUSSELL
PERSONNEL & TRAINING

Visit us online at www.authorsonline.co.uk

An AuthorsOnLine Book

Original art by David Whittington Jones ©
Email davidblackswan@onetel.net.uk

ISBN 0 7552 0129 9

Authors OnLine Ltd
40 Castle Street
Hertford SG14 1HR
England

This book is also available in e-book format, details of which are available at
www.authorsonline.co.uk

Other books by the same author:

101 Tips For Employers

About the Authors

Kate Russell

Some time after qualifying as a barrister, Kate decided that she wasn't cut out for a life of crime. She moved out of court and into industry becoming an operations manager and later specialising as a personnel and training practitioner in the manufacturing, distribution and services sectors. She believes that not being a career personnel advisor from a tender age, but coming at it 'from the round' gives her a pragmatic approach to problem solving in HR. She established Russell Personnel & Training in 1998 and now divides her time between advising small and medium sized businesses on HR issues and delivering a range of highly practical employment law awareness training to line managers. The unusual combination of legal background, direct line management experience and personnel skills, enable Kate to present the stringent requirements of the law balanced against the realities of working life. She is a senior presenter for Employment Law Training Ltd, a popular public speaker and has just completed an MA in Human Resource Management.

Contact details for Russell Personnel & Training

Email: info@Russell-Personnel.com
Web: www.russell-personnel.com
Phone: 01908 261446

If you would like to subscribe to Kate's free e-newsletter, write to subscribe@russell-personnel.com

Kate is the author of "*101 Tips For Employers*"

Derek Eccleston

Derek is an experienced, practical consultant, specialising in the provision of advice and training on employment law and employee relations, through his consultancy Employment Law Training Ltd.

He has spent over 20 years in senior HR roles in a number of industries which include local government, engineering and financial services. Derek works closely with a firm of solicitors and this relationship creates a unique mix of practical awareness, training skills and legal expertise.

He is a Fellow of the Chartered Institute of Personnel and Development (FCIPD), a Chartered Insurer (ACII), and has recently completed an MA in Employment Law with Leicester University. Derek is a senior presenter for the CIPD. He develops and presents public and in-house events for the CIPD as well as other national training organisations, and is also a personal tutor on the Institute's Advanced Certificate in Employment Law.

In 2003 Derek created a website which provides a comprehensive guide for employees and workers on their rights at work (www.yourjobrights.co.uk) and he updates this site regularly. He is the author of HRM Toolkit, published by Gee Publishing and regularly speaks at conferences on employment law issues.

Contact details for Employment Law Ltd

Email: Derek@eltraining.co.uk
Web: www.eltraining.co.uk
Phone: 01789 470700

Acknowledgements

I would like to thank all the people who have encouraged me in this project. Their help and support have been invaluable.

Particular thanks are due to Stuart Gascoyne who agreed to proof the final version of this book with his usual enthusiasm. It was only after reading the book and passing on his comments that he confided that he really hates reading books! Being a very active person, he'd much rather be doing than reading. This, said Stuart, was only the second or third book he'd read since his twenties. Knowing this made me appreciate his efforts even more than I would have done.

Contents

Checklists and Templates

Appendices

Disclaimer

Every effort has been made to ensure that the content of this book is accurate and up to date. No responsibility will be accepted for any inaccuracies found.

It should not be taken as a definitive guide or as a stand-alone document on all aspects of employment law. Professional advice should be sought where appropriate.

Note

For convenience and brevity I have referred to "he" and "him" throughout the book. It is intended to refer to both male and female employees.

Introduction

Businesses call me in when problems are looming. This book came into being because I noticed that nearly always the first words a new client says to me are "Can I sack the b*****d?" or something very similar. The case described below is a fairly typical scenario.

In April 2002 Jim was at the end of his tether. About two years before he'd hired Kevin, a part-qualified accountant, to work in his business. Kevin had never really done a particularly good job, despite lots of pep talks from Jim. Twice he made serious mistakes which could have cost the business a lot of money and embarrassment if they hadn't been picked up in time. Jim didn't like relying on luck to weed out such mistakes and on both occasions spoke to Kevin informally about his work. The final straw came the day Jim found out about another of Kevin's clangers and saw red. The two men had a full and frank discussion, tempers frayed and finally Jim (normally a patient and mild mannered chap) roared "Take this as a formal warning".

Kevin Must Go!

The letter Jim wrote to Kevin after the meeting was headed "Final Written Warning". Jim decided that Kevin must go and consulted me to see what could be done to hasten his departure.

A Little Mistake Which Cou'd Cost The Business £50k

He was dismayed - and surprised - to find that by acting as he had, any attempt to dismiss Kevin in these circumstances meant that Kevin would probably be able to claim unfair dismissal – a little mistake but one which could potentially cost Jim's business £55,000 plus the basic award at employment tribunal. By taking advice Jim started to manage the problem of Kevin's poor performance and reduced the risk of litigation. Kevin is now more careful about his work and Jim's blood pressure is returning to normal.

I wrote this book so that its readers can have a practical resource to give them the answers they need to stay out of trouble. My clients tell me it works for them. I hope it works for you too.

Kate Russell
May 2004

Sobering Statistics

All the way through the 1990s, there was an average of 50,000 applications made to employment tribunals each year. In recent years this has risen dramatically. ACAS reported figures in excess of 130,000 applications being made to tribunals in 2001, although this has reduced slightly since.

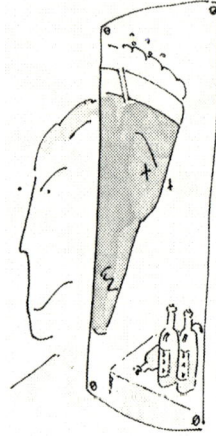

In 1998 compensation increased from a maximum award for unfair dismissal of £12,000 to £50,000.

The statistics provided by ACAS suggest that almost half of the claims made are for unfair dismissal and that ex-employees win just over 40% of those claims.

Is It Just Bad Luck?

Many employers complain that the system is stacked against them. While it's fair to say that employers probably do have to exercise greater reasonableness than employees in most cases, it's equally true to say that where they lose they are often – not always, but often - the authors of their own misfortunes.

The factors most frequently leading to a finding of unfair dismissal against employers include:

❑ The employee was not given the opportunity to defend himself or put forward his side of the story;
❑ The employee was not made aware of all of the evidence against him;
❑ There was no disciplinary hearing;
❑ The investigation of the alleged misconduct or shortcomings was inadequate;
❑ An earlier 'warning' was not made explicit;
❑ The disciplinary procedure was not applied in full;
❑ The procedure used did not follow the employer's own rules;
❑ The employer chose not to have a procedure at all for more senior staff and managers;
❑ The employee was not given a reasonable opportunity to improve performance or conduct;
❑ Insufficient investigation of the medical background in dismissals on grounds of ill health;
❑ The employee had not been given an opportunity to comment on medical evidence in a case of ill-health dismissal.

Section 1   The Purpose Of Discipline

The use of disciplinary procedures is quite common in the UK, and estimates have suggested that around 4% of the working population receive some form of disciplinary sanction each year. But discipline is not all about punishment and retribution.   Sometimes misconduct will be sufficiently serious to justify the termination of employment, but most cases do not involve serious or gross misconduct.   What tends to happen is that where a problem crops up managers don't identify and address the shortfall until it's become a well-established fact. Sometimes they know that there's a problem, but they don't do anything about it in the hope that it will just resolve itself. That might happen occasionally, but usually something has to be done. By this time the thing's been going on for a while, tempers are frayed, patience has expired and managers always want to dismiss. Not only is that potentially an unfair dismissal risk, but it's very wasteful too.

It's worth remembering that the purpose of discipline is to reinforce standards of behaviour and performance. You should help staff to achieve and maintain those standards through guidance and training.   Dismissing unsatisfactory staff without attempting to help them tackle the issue means we have to get rid of them, start the recruitment process again (it costs £1,500 on average to recruit an ordinary staff member, more for senior roles) and train them up again with all the reduced productivity that entails.

If you are grinding your teeth over a difficult staff member, remember that you do have a responsibility – after all, you probably recruited him!

Common Mistakes: The Seven Deadly Sins Of Discipline

1. "Leap frogging". By the time many employers get round to taking formal disciplinary action, they really are in an "I want to sack the b*****d" frame of mind. This tempts them to try to skip stages of the process or attempt to dismiss for a first offence, even when it's not a matter of gross misconduct. You *must* follow the disciplinary procedure. If you don't and you are taken to tribunal you may well find that flawed procedure makes the dismissal unfair.

2 Sometimes known as the "Ostrich Manoeuvre", a favourite strategy for many employers where misconduct or poor performance is concerned is to do nothing. If you want to manage the problem, doing nothing is not an option open to you.

Minor issues dealt with early enough can be nipped in the bud before they become huge, time consuming problems which try your patience. Delay usually makes things worse as the employee may not realise that he is below standard until told about it. He can certainly argue that is the case even if he has a sneaking suspicion that he doesn't meet your requirements. The onus is on you to tell him. Make sure you arrange to speak to the employee as soon as possible – the matter may then be able to be dealt with in an informal way and not as part of the formal disciplinary process.

The main purpose of operating a disciplinary procedure is to encourage improvement in employees whose conduct or performance is below acceptable standards. This is *your* responsibility and you must show that you have fully discharged it.

3   "Where angels fear to tread". Doing nothing or doing nothing for ages is not a good move. We always encourage our managers to act promptly where they see a problem emerging. But please note that there is a difference between acting promptly and following procedures, which is a good thing and dashing in precipitately where angels fear to tread, which is quite another. Before you take any action, you must gather the facts. Even if you find Joe Bloggs with his hands in the till and he confesses that he is in fact robbing you blind, you are still duty bound to follow procedure, suspend Joe, investigate and collect all the facts.

4   Failure to keep proper records is a frequently occurring sin. If there's a problem collect data as soon as possible so that you can clarify what's happened. Gather information before memories fade, including anything the author of the problem has to say. Where it's appropriate to do so take statements from witnesses at the earliest opportunity. Keep records of what is said. You may need to give copies to the offender if the matter goes any further.

5   Making assumptions about your employee is a common fault. It is essential to be fair and – even more important - *be seen to be fair*. Until you have investigated the facts and heard what your employee has to say, you do not know the full picture. Be as objective as possible, keep an open mind, and do not prejudge the issues. You should also consider relevant personal details such as work experience, length of service and any current warnings, as well as any appropriate records and documents.

6   If you are inconsistent in your application of the disciplinary process you may face an unfair dismissal claim. For example, if you have two cases of gross misconduct which are very similar on the facts you may dismiss one offender because you think he's a bit of a trouble maker, but keep the other on a final written warning. The person who has been dismissed may be able to claim unfairness because of your inconsistent application of the sanctions. If the offences are very similar but there are mitigating factors which distinguish the two sets of circumstances, then you may be able to apply different disciplinary sanctions.

7   But ......(There's always a 'But'). The disciplinary process should not be a sausage machine, so while you should be consistent in application, each case must be considered on its own merits within that structure. Personal details such as length of service, past disciplinary history and any current warnings will be relevant. Any decision to discipline an employee must be reasonable in all the

circumstances and must not discriminate on grounds of race, gender, religious belief, sexual orientation or disability.

Getting It Right – What's In It For You?

If you set and publish clear standards and ensure your standards are followed you are much less likely to need to use the formal disciplinary process. In most cases an informal chat where someone transgresses in a minor way will sort out the problem. However, there will always be staff who don't meet your standard after an informal discussion, so there will always be the occasional need to embark upon the formal disciplinary route. Using a fair procedure and applying it fairly will produce the following benefits:

❑ If you manage problems effectively and at an early stage you will need to spend far less time on discipline;
❑ Individual performance improves and efficiency rises;
❑ Disciplinary interviews will be handled effectively;
❑ Disciplinary documentation will be legally sound ;
❑ Appeals against disciplinary penalties will be managed effectively;
❑ Dismissals follow legal guidelines and the risk of an employment tribunal claim is reduced;
❑ You won't have to dismiss so many people therefore there's a reduced need to recruit;
❑ Staff know what will happen if they don't meet company standards and are less likely to transgress.

Employment law has developed dramatically in the last few years. It is a complex matter and applies to all employers, irrespective of size. There are few amnesties for small businesses. The upper limit for unfair dismissal is over £50,000 and increases annually but employers are often unaware of the risks.

Discipline and dismissal is potentially a very serious matter if we get it wrong, but just to get some perspective, while there are some well-publicised cases with high levels of compensation, the average award is about £4,000. If you can show that you've done most things right, compensation can be very much reduced.

The main cost is not so much the level of compensation if you lose, but the many hours of preparation time that you have to spend getting ready to fight a case. While you don't have to use solicitors to defend your case, many employers do and the costs can be high. Tribunals have a nasty habit of postponing cases at the last minute too, so you might find that you and all your witnesses have travelled to a tribunal to present your case and then it's postponed with half an hour's notice. All of this deflects you from your proper job which is running the business.

You are required by law to have disciplinary (if you have more than 20 staff) and grievance procedures. A failure to follow those procedures will almost certainly result in an unfair dismissal. The main reason that employers lose at tribunal is their failure to follow their own disciplinary procedures.

Section 2 Statutory Rights

Employment Rights Act 1996

The Employment Rights Act 1996 creates a legal obligation for any employer with 20 or more employees to include details of the disciplinary rules within the written statement of employment particulars.

"Is this the act of a reasonable employer?"

Employment Rights (Disputes Resolution) Act 1998

The Act puts much more emphasis on the need for employers and employees to make full use of internal procedures and seek a conciliated settlement rather than go forward to an employment tribunal. In particular, the Act recommends that employees and employers should make full use of the internal appeals procedure in dismissal cases. Tribunals have the power to reduce the compensation to employees who are offered an opportunity to appeal, but who go direct to the Tribunal Service. It also gives tribunals the power to increase the financial compensation to employees who are not offered an appeal against dismissal.

The 1998 Act gave ACAS the power to prepare and operate an arbitration scheme for unfair dismissal cases. The scheme is voluntary and applies only if both parties agree. It does not apply to claims for constructive dismissal or to other claims raised at the same time as an unfair dismissal claim. In entering into the scheme, both parties give up any right of appeal.

If the arbitrator finds that the dismissal was unfair, an order for reinstatement, re-engagement or compensation will be made.

It has not been used very much. Only a small number of cases have been heard this way.

Statutory Dispute Resolution

Many small employers who have fewer than 20 staff don't bother to have written disciplinary rules or procedure. This can lead to confusion in the way in which problems are handled. It's important to remember that even though there may be no legal requirement to have a written disciplinary process, there is no small employer exemption from the unfair dismissal provisions. The numbers of unfair dismissal applications arising from small businesses have been so marked that the

Government decided to introduce a basic statutory framework for dispute management. The Employment Act 2002 introduced the concept of a statutory dispute resolution process to try to stem the flood of claims being made to tribunal. It is likely to be introduced in the autumn of 2004. The purpose of the statutory process is to help to build constructive employment relations and reduce the need for litigation. It aims to encourage internal resolution of workplace disputes by:

- Introducing minimum internal disciplinary and grievance procedures;
- Encouraging employees to raise grievances with their employer before applying to the tribunal;
- Providing a limited extension to time limits for lodging a tribunal complaint to allow procedures to be concluded;
- Allowing variation of tribunal awards to support use of the procedures.
- Facilitating better understanding of the employment relationship through wider compliance with the written statement of employment particulars and removal of the 20-employee threshold on provision of information on disciplinary and grievance procedures.
- Altering the way unfair dismissals are judged so that, provided the minimum standards set out in the Act are met and the dismissal is otherwise fair, procedural shortcomings can be disregarded. Employers will always have to follow the basic procedures, but will no longer be penalised for irrelevant mistakes beyond that - provided the dismissal would otherwise be fair. This means that the dismissal must have been for a fair reason and the employer must have acted reasonably in treating it as a reason for dismissing the employee.
- Providing for timely and amicable settlement through fixed conciliation.
- Providing for efficient, swifter delivery of tribunal services through practice directions, management of weak cases, revision of the costs regime and mandatory tribunal forms.

The statutory dispute resolution procedures will form the minimum standard although better contractual procedures will not be affected. If an employer fails to follow the statutory Disciplinary and Dismissal Procedure (DDP) a dismissal will automatically be unfair (the employee must have a year's service qualification). The procedures only include employees, but not wider categories of workers.

Following consultation the Government has set out its conclusions on key issues:

- 'Disciplinary action' will not be extended to require an employer to activate the three stage standard procedure before issuing warnings or suspensions on full pay. Such actions may give rise to a grievance in respect of which the statutory grievance procedures apply.

- 'Grievance' is defined as a 'complaint by an employee about action which his employer has taken or is considering taking in relation to him'.

- In most cases the statutory grievance procedures will apply where the employment has ended. There are a number of exceptions to this, for example, where there has been a sudden and unforeseen cessation of a business or where an employee cannot continue in employment without breaching a legal duty or restriction, the statutory procedures will not apply.

- Where the subject matter of the employee's grievance would also give rise to a claim in an employment tribunal, the time limit for bringing that claim is automatically extended to six months once the grievance procedure has started.

- The time limit for bringing a claim in respect of disciplinary action or dismissal will be extended where the employee has reasonable grounds for believing the disciplinary process is ongoing when the normal time limit expires.

Note that even though you are not required by the statutory process to use the three stage standard procedure before issuing warnings, the ACAS code is still considered to be best practice, so it will be sensible to ensure that no warning are issued until you have fully investigated and held a disciplinary hearing to allow the employee to put his version of events.

Standard Disciplinary And Dismissal Procedures

Step 1:Statement of grounds for action and invitation to meeting

(1) The employer must set out in writing the employee's alleged conduct or characteristics, or other circumstances, which lead him to contemplate dismissing or taking disciplinary action against the employee.
(2) The employer must send the statement or a copy of it to the employee and invite the employee to attend a meeting to discuss the matter. The employee must be advised of his right to be accompanied.

Step 2: Meeting

(1) The meeting must take place before action is taken, except in the case where the disciplinary action consists of suspension.
(2) The meeting must not take place unless-
(a) the employer has informed the employee what the basis was for including in the statement the ground or grounds given in it; and
(b) the employee has had a reasonable opportunity to consider his response to that information.
(3) The employee must take all reasonable steps to attend the meeting.
(4) After the meeting, the employer must inform the employee of his decision and notify him of the right to appeal against the decision if he is not satisfied with it.

Step 3: Appeal

(1) If the employee does wish to appeal, he must inform the employer.
(2) If the employee informs the employer of his wish to appeal, the employer must invite him to attend a further meeting. The employer must remind the employee of his right to be accompanied.
(3) The employee must take all reasonable steps to attend the meeting.
(4) The appeal meeting need not take place before the dismissal or disciplinary action takes effect. The appeal should be to a different manager where possible.
(5) After the appeal meeting, the employer must inform the employee of his final decision.

Modified Disciplinary And Dismissal Procedure

The modified procedure should be used when an employee has been summarily dismissed for misconduct or has already left employment.

Step 1: Statement of grounds for action

(1) The employer must set out in writing:

(i) the employee's alleged misconduct which has led to the dismissal;
(ii) what the basis was for thinking at the time of the dismissal that the employee was guilty of the alleged misconduct; and
(iii) the employee's right to appeal against dismissal.

(2) He must send the statement or a copy of it to the employee.

Step 2: Appeal

(1) If the employee does wish to appeal, he must inform the employer.
(2) If the employee informs the employer of his wish to appeal, the employer must invite him to attend a meeting.
(3) The employee must take all reasonable steps to attend the meeting.
(4) After the appeal meeting, the employer must inform the employee of his final decision.

Statutory Grievance Procedures

Statutory Grievance Procedures (GPs) are subject to the same general requirements as DDPs in that:

❑ Each step and action under the procedure must be taken without unreasonable delay;
❑ Timing and location of meetings must be reasonable;
❑ Meetings must be conducted in a manner that enables both employer and employee to explain their cases.

In the case of appeal meetings that are not first meetings, the employer should, so far as is reasonably practical, be represented by a more senior manager than attended the first meeting (unless the most senior manager attended that meeting).

Standard Grievance Procedures

Step 1: Statement of grievance

The employee must set out the grievance in writing and send that statement, or a copy of it, to the employer.

Step 2: Meeting

The employer must invite the employee to attend a meeting to discuss the grievance.
The meeting must not take place unless:
a) the employee has informed the employer what the basis for the grievance was when he made the statement as required by Step 1; and
b) the employer has had a reasonable opportunity to consider his response to that information.
The employee must take all reasonable steps to attend the meeting. After the meeting the employer must inform the employee of his decision in response to the grievance and notify the employee of the right to appeal against the decision if he is not satisfied.

Step 3: Appeal

If the employee does want to appeal, he must inform the employer.
If the employee informs the employer of his wish to appeal, the employer must invite the employee to attend a further meeting.
After the appeal meeting the employer must inform the employee of his final decision.
A modified version of the standard GP is available.

Modified Grievance Procedure

Step 1: Statement of grievance.

The employee must:
a) Set out in writing - (i) the grievance, and (ii) the basis for it; and
b) Send the statement, or a copy of it to the employer.

Step 2: Response

The employer must set out his response in writing and send the statement or a copy of it to the employee.

The modified procedure is intended for use in circumstances where the employee has already left employment. A typical example would be in cases of constructive dismissal, where it would be inappropriate for an employee to return to work to discuss the issues in person with the employer.

Employees who do not comply with this procedure will be unable to present a claim to an employment tribunal in relation to the subject of their grievance. So before bringing a tribunal claim the employee must have written to the employer setting out the grievance and the basis for it. This must be done 28 days before any claim can be lodged.

Right To Be Accompanied

Any employee or worker who attends a disciplinary or grievance hearing has a right to be accompanied by a work place colleague or trade union representative. Employees have no statutory right to be accompanied by their mum or dad (unless they work in the business) or their solicitor.

If the companion is a trade union representative from outside the business, always check his identification before starting the process.

The legislation describes the person accompanying the employee as a "companion" rather than a "representative", so his role is to accompany the employee at the meeting to offer support and make representations on behalf of the individual. He may confer with the employee during the hearing but may not speak in his place.

If the chosen companion is not available at the time you propose to hold the hearing, you should reschedule. The person to be taken through the disciplinary hearing should suggest an alternative time to meet which is both reasonable and falls before the end of five working days after the date originally set for the hearing.

The ACAS Code

ACAS is the Advisory, Conciliation and Arbitration Service. Founded in 1974 it is a public body funded by tax payers. Its purpose is to provide three main services:

Conciliation

ACAS brings together the parties in a dispute with the aim of moving forward to a settlement acceptable to all sides.

Arbitration

ACAS acts as an independent arbitrator or arbiter (in Scotland) deciding the outcome of a dispute. The decision may well be binding in law.

Mediation

ACAS acts as an intermediary in talking to both sides. The aim is for the parties to resolve the problem between themselves but the mediator will make suggestions along the way.

It has provided a number of guidelines which don't have the force of law but, like the Highway Code, are seen to define best practice. The ACAS Disciplinary Code is used by employment tribunals as a benchmark. If your procedures include the following key points and you follow them, you significantly reduce the risk of a claim of unfair dismissal. Failure to follow a procedure prescribed in the code can make an otherwise fair dismissal unfair.

When drawing up and applying disciplinary procedures you should have regard to the requirements of natural justice. This means you must not only be fair, you must also be seen to be fair. You must be reasonable and consistent in your approach.

You can look at the full code of practice by logging on to the ACAS website (www.acas.org.uk).

According to the code a disciplinary procedure should:

- ❑ Be in writing;
- ❑ Specify to whom they apply if there are different rules for different groups;
- ❑ Be non-discriminatory;
- ❑ Provide for matters to be dealt with quickly;
- ❑ Ensure that individuals are made fully aware of what their disciplinary offence is;
- ❑ State the type of disciplinary action and who can take it;
- ❑ Ensure that disciplinary action is not taken until the case has been carefully investigated;
- ❑ Provide for a full hearing which gives individuals an opportunity to state their case;
- ❑ Provide for proceedings, witness statements and records to be kept confidential (to the parties concerned);
- ❑ Allow individuals to be accompanied by a union representative or a colleague;
- ❑ Not allow dismissal for a first offence (except for gross misconduct);
- ❑ Ensure an explanation is given for disciplinary action;
- ❑ Specify an appeals procedure.

In addition, your disciplinary procedures should:

- Apply to all employees, irrespective of their length of service, status or number of hours worked;
- Ensure that suspension for investigation prior to the disciplinary hearing is with pay. Any period of suspension should be brief, and should never be used as a sanction against the employee prior to a disciplinary hearing and decision;
- Ensure that the employee will be heard in good faith and that there is no pre-judgement of the issue;
- Ensure that, where the facts are in dispute, no disciplinary penalty is imposed until the case has been carefully investigated, and there is a reasonably held belief that the employee committed the act in question.

The Reasonable Employer

Let me introduce you to the fictional legal character known as the Reasonable Employer. This is the test against which your behaviour and decisions will be measured. The reasonableness of your response will vary, depending on the situation and the relevant facts. The test is whether a reasonable employer in the same employment situation would also have done the same as you.

Some help is given by the court's guidelines laid down in *British Home Stores v Burchell* which says that:

- The employer must have a genuine belief that the employee has committed the act of misconduct;

- The belief must be based upon reasonable grounds;

- The employer must have carried out as much investigation as was reasonable into all the circumstances of the case.

As the stronger party in an employment contract the employer always has to demonstrate a higher level of reasonableness than the employee. So you must show transparency and reasonableness in your actions and show that you have put yourself in the other person's shoes, taken all relevant factors into account, taken advice, discussed the issues with the employee and considered all possible alternatives. In other words you have to be able to justify your actions.

Section 3   Avoiding Problems

Set Standards

A standard is the minimum level of conduct or performance acceptable to the company setting it. In my experience most managers communicate standards very poorly (where they do it at all). Have you ever given an instruction to an employee in a way that you thought was absolutely crystal clear and then found he'd done something entirely different? Most of the time, that lack of clarity is our own fault. It might be that we're short of time so we skipped giving full details, that we've given incorrect information, that we've missed a bit of relevant information out, we've made assumptions about levels of knowledge or understanding or a variety of other things. The end result is that something is done incorrectly or not at all. That can be pretty frustrating and we risk another "Sack The B*****d" situation.

It's your job as a manager to communicate the standards you require clearly. It is essential that you tell your staff in specific and measurable terms what it is you require of them in the way of behaviour and performance. As human beings we are not by nature very specific in our conversational speech. I commonly hear managers say things like, "You must be here on time." And then they're surprised when employees come sauntering in ten or fifteen minutes late. If you think about it, that's an almost meaningless remark. Don't expect employees to automatically interpret your statements in the way you mean them. We talk very generally, but to get the results you want you must learn to be more precise and detailed. It would be more effective to say "You must be at your work-station prepared to start work at 8am."

So try to express standards using the S-M-A-R-T formula.

S   = Specific
M   = Measurable
A   = Achievable
R   = Realistic
T   = Time scale

If you just bumble along, talking very non-specifically, you are likely to get what you asked for but not what you want. This does take a bit of practice, but it's worth while when you get the results you want.

"I can't see anything wrong"

Example: a manager interviewed a female employee about her appalling attendance record. She'd taken about 20 days sickness in a few months. He warned her that if she did not improve, she would be taken through the disciplinary process for non-attendance and would ultimately be dismissed. They agreed to meet in another three months. At the second meeting the manager discovered that

she had indeed improved – she had taken 15 days of sickness absence, not 20!
What he should have said was something along the lines of "If you are off work
more than x days during the next three months I will talk to you again as part of
our formal disciplinary procedure."

Checklist Standards

It is virtually impossible to bring about an improvement in someone's
performance or conduct unless the following elements are present. Unless an
employee is prepared to acknowledge that he was aware of a standard, and
there is clear evidence that he is below the standard, you are unlikely to achieve
a successful conclusion. Make sure:

❑   The organisation has a clear set of standards;

❑   The standards have been communicated to all workers;

❑   Factual evidence is available which indicates that conduct or performance
    is below the accepted standard;

❑   There are clear rules and procedures, which outline to all employees how
    the issue will be dealt with.

❑   Standards are S-M-A-R-T, wherever possible.

You must also be very clear about what will happen if employees don't meet the
standard. Tell them they'll be taken through the disciplinary process. It's not
supposed to be a threat, but you do have a duty to advise them very clearly about
the final outcome of repeated breaches. There should never be any nasty surprises
for employees when it comes to discipline.

Managers always complain (usually bitterly and at length) about the amount of
time it takes them to properly manage discipline. If you don't want to have to
spend so much time on it the answer's in your hands. Get your standards across
clearly at the earliest possible opportunity, reinforce them and act promptly if
there's a breach. There's an unspoken message here too. You will find that if staff
know what's expected of them and they know that transgressions are firmly dealt
with they are much less likely to misbehave.

You have no right to complain that your staff don't meet your requirements if
you have never clearly told them what it is you require. I have known staff
dismissed (and reinstated) because they were in breach of a rule that they didn't
know existed. The manager's explanation? "He should have known, he's been
here long enough."

Make Life Easier For Yourself

Be selective at recruitment. Be honest about what is expected of staff and tell them about key standards, for example, a requirement to wear a uniform or work shifts. These should be confirmed in your offer letter or staff handbook. The earlier that prospective staff learn about the standards expected of them, the less chance there is that there will be problems later on. Always – *always*! - take up references. It's so much easier to avoid problems if you don't recruit them into your business in the first place. (See next page for employment reference request)

So not only is it is good practice to tell prospective employees of your key standards at the recruitment stage, it will save you a lot of time. Reinforce those standards at induction, on a daily or weekly basis in the workplace and at appraisal.

You should always carry out some form of induction for new members of staff. This is recommended by the ACAS Code and in health and safety legislation. It has the dual benefit of helping them settle in, and bringing them up to speed with their work more rapidly. Keep records of what you cover at induction. An induction checklist covering the key points can be useful and it also gives you a record of what you discussed at induction. See example on page 18.

If you hold appraisals or performance reviews these can be useful opportunities to remind staff about standards and review performance and conduct, although they must not degenerate into a disciplinary discussion.

Many companies require staff to work a probationary period at the beginning of their employment. If you do that, don't forget to review their performance during probation. Don't wait to the end of the probation to break it to the staff member that he hasn't come up to scratch. You may have to extend the period of probation if necessary. Unless otherwise stated, you should still follow your disciplinary procedure. Note that when the statutory discipline and dismissal procedures become effective, the employee will have the right to go through a basic form of discipline from the first day of employment.

Disciplinary Rules

Rules set standards of conduct and performance at work and make clear to employees what is expected of them. If they are to achieve the organisation's standards, staff need to know what they are. Rules must be clearly communicated to all employees so that everyone knows what is expected from them and what will happen if they don't comply. Please don't assume that because you know what the rules are that everyone else does too.

Employment Reference Request

Name of applicant: ....

Job title: ....
The above applicant states that he worked for your company between [date] and
[date] as a [...].
Would you confirm that this was so and let us know whether in your opinion
he/she performed his/her tasks competently and conscientiously.

....
Reason he/ she left employment

....
No. of days of sickness absence in last three years. Please show reasons for
sickness absence.

....
Were there any disciplinary warnings live on his/her file at the termination of
employment? If so please give brief details.

....
Was the employee the subject of disciplinary proceedings at the time he/she left
the company?

	Satisfactory	Unsatisfactory	Comment
Relationships with other staff, customers & suppliers			
Timekeeping			

Name: (Please print) ....

Signature ....

Position ....

Date ....

Checklist – Induction Training Record

Name: Start date:

Dept:

Item	Signature of employee	Date	Manager's Initials
Tour of premises			
Fire evacuation procedures & assembly point			
Introduction to First Aiders			
Introduction to management & colleagues			
Outline of products			
General safety procedures			
Protective clothing			
H&S policy			
P45, NI number, next of kin details, bank details			
Terms & conditions			
Pay arrangements			
Holidays			
Disciplinary procedure			
Sickness absence reporting			
Job description			
Attendance requirements			
Timekeeping			
Performance			
Use of company equipment			
Sales/ productivity targets			

Examples of disciplinary rules commonly include:

- Timekeeping
- Attendance
- Performance
- Appearance
- Conduct
- Health and safety rules

They are more likely to be effective and accepted if they are reasonable and staff understand the rationale.

Rules should be:

- Written down to ensure that everyone understands what is required of them;
- Non-discriminatory in content and applied irrespective of sex, marital status, racial group, disability, age, religion or sexual orientation;
- Well publicised and readily available – managers should take all reasonable steps to ensure that everyone knows and understands them.

It's important to cover company rules as part of the induction programme when new staff join the business. Special attention should be paid to ensure that rules are understood by employees with little experience of working life (for instance young people or those returning to work after a lengthy break), and by employees whose English or reading ability is limited or impaired by disability.

Example: C, a delegate at a training session, told the following story about working with young people showing how important it is to spell out rules. She runs a tea-shop and employs several staff between the ages of 16-18 at the weekends and in the school holidays. C said jokingly that she was thinking about making the wearing of Wellies compulsory safety wear! Despite the fact that there were safety notices in the kitchen and all staff received safety training, there was always someone who would still prod teacakes caught in the toaster with a metal knife while the toaster was still plugged in and switched on. Some teenagers don't appear to be on the same planet as most of us.

Where a rule has fallen into disuse or has not been applied consistently, make sure you tell employees before you make any changes in practice.

Rules do need to be revised from time to time as society, technology and legislation change. For example, most companies now have rules about internet and email use. This technology is a relatively recent development, almost unheard of ten years ago. Any revisions to the rules should be communicated quickly to all employees, and they should be issued with a revised written statement within one month of the change.

When the statutory discipline and dismissal procedures become effective you should review your procedures to make sure that they comply.

Section 4   When Is It Fair To Dismiss?

At law there are five fair reasons for dismissal.

1.   Capability – "Can't"

This is split into several areas.

- ❑ Qualifications - does the employee have the necessary qualifications for the job and is a particular qualification actually needed for this type of job?
- ❑ Incompetence - this can be repeated minor incompetence or a very serious individual incident.
- ❑ Ill health - an employee who is genuinely ill on a regular or long term basis.

Qualification

If an employee loses or fails to achieve a qualification necessary to do his job he may be dismissed on grounds of capability. However, this is not automatically fair and you should not dismiss until you have explored all the alternative ways of trying to accommodate him. So, for example, if a sales representative whose job it is to travel to clients or prospects loses his driver's licence for a year, you should consider the options. Can he work from home or from the office? Can his work be adjusted so that he travels by public transport? Can he have a driver? Can he do another job in the business while his licence is withheld?

Incompetence

Capability on grounds of ill health

Performance is one the most frequent reasons for discipline and one of the least well done. It's your job to show that poor performance is the reason for the dismissal and that you reasonably believe your employee is not capable of working to the standard you require. It would not be fair to dismiss for a first breach if the incompetence is minor. It has to be really serious, for example, a life-threatening action or omission. You must do everything reasonable to help him meet the required standard of performance. This normally takes the form of coaching, ιe-training, giving a reasonable amount of time to improve (two months rather than two weeks) and generally supporting the employee. You must formally warn the employee before dismissal and advise him of the consequences of failure to improve.

In deciding whether an employer was reasonable in dismissing for incompetence it may be relevant to know whether appropriate training was given.

Example -minor incompetence: A woman was dismissed for assembling 471 out of 500 components incorrectly. She claimed this was the way she had been shown how to assemble them. The chargehand denied ever having shown her how to do it. Either way the employer was damned, for either she had been wrongly trained or not trained at all. Davidson v Kent Meters [1975]

Example - gross incompetence: T was a pilot who crash-landed a passenger plane in good flying conditions. Nobody was hurt, but the plane was badly damaged. After a full investigation and disciplinary hearing T was dismissed for gross incompetence. He complained that as he had an unblemished record he should not have been dismissed for a first offence.

The Court of Appeal upheld the decision to dismiss saying that in some professions the degree of skill needed was so high and the likely consequences of deviation from that level of skill potentially so serious that it would be fair to dismiss in a first instance. Alidair v Taylor [1978]

Checklist Managing Performance

- ❑ Identify the performance issue in specific terms. For example, sales targets are set at £50,000 sales per month. The rest of the team is meeting this target. The employee whose performance we wish to discuss is achieving an average of £30,000.

- ❑ Investigate the problem. Have informal discussions taken place? If so, are there any notes?

- ❑ Write to the employee giving details of the issues and arranging a disciplinary hearing giving up to five days notice.

- ❑ Warn the employee if it is appropriate to do so.

- ❑ Agree an action plan, targets and objectives. Identify whether there are any training needs.

- ❑ Set a reasonable time for improvement. If you are to be fair you should allow a reasonable time to improve – months rather than weeks. Tell the employee what the consequences will be if he doesn't meet the required performance standard.

- ❑ Monitor progress.

- ❑ Offer the employee the right to appeal against any disciplinary penalty.

Ill Health

It is fair to dismiss an employee who is no longer capable of working because he is too unwell to do so. If your staff receive company sick pay as a contractual benefit the dismissal should not become effective until the sick pay is exhausted or paid in lieu. In cases of long term ill health you should concentrate on investigating into the medical facts and consulting with the affected employee about the available options. In these circumstances it is not appropriate to go through any lengthy disciplinary or warnings procedure.

Since 1995 the Disability Discrimination Act has placed an additional obligation upon employers to consider alternatives to dismissal where the ill health is caused through an illness which is defined as a disability. If the employee may be disabled within the definition of the Act, there is a requirement to consider making reasonable adjustments to the work or the workplace.

A person may be disabled within the meaning of the Disability Discrimination Act if he has a physical or mental impairment which is substantial and has a long term adverse effect on his ability to carry out normal day to day activities.

It is incumbent upon you to consider all the alternatives to dismissal. It may be possible to find an alternative job or change the job content to accommodate the employee's changed requirements. This may not be possible, so a fair procedure before dismissal would include the following:

❑ Discuss the employee's current state of health and the likelihood of a return to work within a reasonable period with him.
❑ You can also ask about what alternative work he may be able to do. Gain the employee's permission to talk to his doctor, and arrange to obtain a medical opinion. If the doctor is unwilling or unable to give an opinion as to when the employee will be able to return to work, ask for him to be examined by a third party.
❑ Always involve and consult the employee at all stages.
❑ When you have the medical opinion, and it is still clear that the employee is unlikely to be able to return to work discuss the steps the company proposes to take with him.
❑ If the employee is not likely to return, serve proper notice of termination of employment.
❑ Offer the right of appeal against the dismissal.

Some companies have a capability procedure which is distinct from the disciplinary procedure covering conduct. There is an example of an absence management procedure at the back of the book.

In your role as the Reasonable Employer you have to be seen to be properly considering all the options and going through a fair procedure. If you don't, you may end up with an unfair dismissal claim, even if the end result would have been the same anyway, fair procedure or no fair procedure.

Example: D had been employed by the Local Authority since 1959. He was aged 56. He had had a history of ill health, and at the time of his dismissal, had been off sick for five full months.

The employer wrote to the District Community Physician and asked him to indicate whether D's ill health was such that he should be retired on the grounds of ill health. The District Community Physician asked another doctor to examine D and produce reports. On the basis of this report from a second physician, the District Community Physician wrote to D and dismissed him. The Employment Appeal Tribunal (EAT) found that the employer had failed to consult with D and had failed to obtain the medical position so that they could make an informed decision to dismiss. He had therefore been unfairly dismissed. East Lindsey District Council v Daubney [1977]

Medical Reports

If you want to write to an employee's own doctor, you must ask for his written permission. If you refer him to your company's occupational health advisor, you don't need written permission from the employee provided that your terms and conditions of employment state that you have the right to require the employee to undergo a medical examination.

The Access to Medical Reports Act 1988 allows a person to have access to a medical report about him if it is prepared by his own doctor. The employee has the right to state that he wishes to have access to the report. Additionally he can withhold consent to the report being supplied to the employer or request amendments to the report.

Where the employee states that he wishes to have access to the report, the employer must let the GP know this when making the application and at the same time let the employee know that the report has been requested. The employee won't be able to access the report if it is prepared by a specialist or company doctor who has not had any responsibility for his medical care.

Employers are under a duty to get medical evidence upon which to base their decisions. You will find that you need to write extremely detailed questions if you are to obtain any really useful medical evidence. Doctors are naturally very cautious and won't give very firm answers unless you specify what you want to know. A sample letter is shown on the next page and the accompanying questionnaire on page 25.

Sample Letter To Doctor

Mr. A Smith
Kings Hospital
Kings Beeching
Northants
NN8 1SD

21st July 2003

Dear Mr Smith

**JOANNE BROWN, 4 THE TERRACE, KINGS BEECHING,
NORTHANTS, NN8 2RG, DOB: 6.8.65**

Joanne Brown has been employed by Easi-Buy Ltd as an Administration
Supervisor since August 2000. She supervises a small team who process
orders placed by customers. They also prepare and send out invoices. Joanne
is office-based most of the time. She occasionally visits customers at their
premises.

I understand that she has been referred to you for investigation and
treatment of her symptoms which she has described to us as, primarily, severe
abdominal pains. She has given us permission to write to you as she has been
suffering significant periods of ill health (see enclosed statement of
permission).

We are keen to do what we can to help her. In a recent discussion, we
elicited that she feels more unwell in the early morning and have therefore
agreed with her that she may start work an hour later.

Joanne has told us that she has been undergoing a series of tests for food
intolerance and a range of other conditions, including Crohn's Disease and
irritable bowel syndrome. She has also been considering asking to be put on
an elimination diet.

We need to find out more about her condition, to decide what is the best
course of action and what we can do to help.

Attached is a questionnaire and an addressed pre-paid envelope. I would
be grateful if you could complete these as fully as possible. Please contact me
on 01844 511511 if you have any queries.

Thank you very much for your assistance in this matter. I look forward to
hearing from you.

Yours sincerely

Mrs Jayne Joyce
Finance Director
Enc :

MEDICAL QUESTIONNAIRE

NAME: JOANNE BROWN

1   Please give your opinion regarding the general state of Joanne's health.

2   Please specify the medical condition from which she is suffering.

3   Please advise on the timescale for her recovery.

4   What has Joanne been tested for?

5   What were the test outcomes?

6   What treatment has she received?

7   Is she receiving treatment now? If so, please specify what.

8   Will she be able to continue to work in her present job role, either full time or part time?

9   If Joanne is unable to continue in her present job role, what type of duties might she be able to undertake?

10   What special needs might arise?

11   What in your view can we do to help her?

12   Any other general comments

Name: ....

Signature: ....

Date: ....

2.   Conduct – "Won't"

Here are some of the possible situations where an employee's conduct may have given you good reason to dismiss him:

- ❑   Theft
- ❑   Corruption, including taking bribes
- ❑   Being drunk at work
- ❑   Taking drugs at work
- ❑   Abusive behaviour
- ❑   Leaking confidential documents or information
- ❑   Hacking into computer files - this includes stealing passwords
- ❑   Being absent from work on a regular basis
- ❑   Constantly late for work
- ❑   Unsuitable work clothes or appearance
- ❑   Taking holidays without permission
- ❑   Unsuitable conduct with other members of staff during office hours
- ❑   Unsuitable conduct outside work hours that has an impact on the employee's job or brings the employer into disrepute

Note that your policy should distinguish between gross and serious misconduct.

Short Term Sickness Absence

While long term sickness absence is usually handled as a capability matter, frequent and persistent short-term absence often comes under the heading of conduct. It's not so much questioning sickness absence as tackling non-attendance issues. An examination of records will identify those employees who are regularly absent and may show an absence pattern. In such cases you should make sufficient enquiries to determine whether the absence is because of genuine illness or for other reasons. If there is an underlying medical reason for the short term absence it will still be a capability matter.

Investigate unexpected absences promptly and ask your employee for an explanation at a return-to-work interview.   If he doesn't come up with an acceptable reason, treat the matter as a conduct issue and deal with it under the disciplinary procedure.

In many cases there will be no medical certificate to support frequent short-term, self-certified, absences. You may be harbouring dark suspicions but you're not a doctor so you still need to investigate the matter. Ask the employee to see a doctor to establish whether treatment is necessary and whether the underlying reason for the absence is work-related. If there's no underlying medical reason for the absences take action under the disciplinary procedure for non-attendance. Never accuse staff of skiving or malingering.

If the absence could be disability related, the Disability Discrimination Act requires you to think about what reasonable adjustments could be made in the workplace to help the employee.   This might be something as simple as an adequate, ergonomic chair, or a power-assisted piece of equipment. Reasonable adjustment also means redeployment to a different type of work if necessary.

Example: T had been employed by W Ltd since 1979. She was employed with 14 other staff on a shift which required flexibility in the sense that everyone on the shift had to be able to do all the jobs. She had a club foot, which resulted in progressive disturbance in her bone structure. This caused her problems with sciatica and other symptoms of pain and discomfort at work which made it difficult for her to stand for long periods of time. Some of the jobs on this shift requred long periods of standing.

From 1995 onwards T's performance and attendance record began to deteriorate significantly. W Ltd wrote to the company doctor, and asked for guidance about her condition. They also received expert advice which indicated that a specially designed chair might help T. The chair would cost around £1,000, but was available free of charge for a four week trial period. W Ltd did not obtain the chair but provided T with a variety of ordinary chairs, none of which met her particular needs. In January 1997 T was dismissed for "poor performance". She brought a claim under the Disability Discrimination Act and claimed that she had been unfairly dismissed. The tribunal found that W Ltd had failed to make reasonable adjustment and accordingly she was unfairly dismissed. Tarling v Wisdom Toothbrushes Ltd [1997]

If the absence is because of temporary problems relating to dependents, the employee may be entitled to have unpaid time off. Employees have the right to reasonable time off to deal with an emergency involving a dependent.

If the absence is because the employee has difficulty managing both work and home responsibilities then you should give serious consideration to more flexible ways of working. From April 2003 employees with young (up to the age of six) and disabled (up to the age of eighteen) children have had the right to request flexible working arrangements. This includes job-sharing, part-time working, flexi-time, working from home/ teleworking and term time contracts. An employer who refuses an application to work flexibly must have a good business reason for doing so.

In all cases the employee should be told what improvement in attendance is expected and warned of the likely consequences if this does not happen. If there is no improvement, you should take the employee's length of service, performance, the likelihood of a change in attendance, the availability of suitable alternative work, and the effect of past and future absences on the organisation into account in deciding appropriate action.

Conduct or Capability?

Capability and conduct should be treated separately. You need to recognise the difference between warning someone for a capability matter and warning him for his conduct. If you fail to distinguish between the two, you are much more likely to run the risk of a successful unfair dismissal application. As previously stated some organisations have separate disciplinary procedures for dealing with capability and conduct, but this is a matter of choice for the individual organisation.

It is important that any dismissal proceedings, and all the disciplinary penalties to that point, distinguish clearly between breaches of performance standards and conduct issues.

This means that where your employee already has a warning for misconduct, and then demonstrates a lack of capability, you should issue him with a first warning for the capability matter, quite separate from the misconduct.

3. Redundancy

You must have a fair procedure for selecting whose job is going to be made redundant. Once the method has been decided upon you should stick to it. One of the most commonly used methods is "last in - first out", but increasingly employers are using a range of criteria such as attendance, time-keeping, disciplinary record, knowledge, experience and qualifications to make their selection. You cannot select an employee for redundancy if it is based upon one of the unfair dismissal exceptions.

Many employers still look upon redundancy as their "get out of jail free" card. However, if an employee can raise a doubt that the redundancy is really for some other reason, he can claim unfair dismissal.

Example: S was selected for redundancy while on maternity leave. She claimed that the reason she had been chosen was because of her pregnancy and brought a sex discrimination and unfair dismissal application. Selection for redundancy for a reason related to pregnancy or maternity would make the dismissal automatically unfair. The tribunal accepted her argument and she was awarded 2.5 years salary and 10 years worth of pension contributions, an award which cost the company £163,000. Brentwood Bros(Manchester) Ltd v Shepherd [2003]

4. Statute

If to continue to employ someone would mean that you are breaking the law, then it will be fair to dismiss. For example if you employ a foreign employee whose work permit has expired, to continue to employ him would break the immigration laws and this is a criminal matter. However, you should check whether the situation can be made legal before dismissing the employee.

5. Some Other Substantial Reason (S.O.S.R.)

This is very wide and is used to cover virtually every other possible reason. For example, where a company is being reorganised for valid and serious business reasons and some employees refuse to reorganise along with it or where they are no longer considered suitable. In one case an employee who refused to use computers when they were installed, despite receiving training, was dismissed. This was said to be a valid reason to dismiss.

Example: C was part of an attempted management buy-out which lost to another company. All the directors except C resigned and the new board voted to remove him. C claimed that terminating his contract of service as Chief Executive was unfair dismissal. The court decided that the dismissal came within the meaning of S.O.S.R. It was clear a new board would not want a Chief Executive who had been voted off and C knew he risked losing his job. Cobley v Forward Technology Industries Ltd [2003]

Section 5   The Importance Of Procedure

Getting procedural matters right in disciplinary matters is critical. So much so that a procedural flaw can render a dismissal unfair, even where the person's dismissal would otherwise have been fair. The tribunal will ask two questions about a dismissal. Firstly, was the dismissal for a fair reason? And if it was, was the dismissal dealt with fairly? This means that an employer can dismiss an employee for a perfectly valid reason, but the way in which it was handled was unfair and so an unfair dismissal claim can be made.

Example: H had been employed as manager of the George Inn, Southwark since 1985. He was a very successful manager, having won the Evening Standard Pub of the Year Award and received many letters of congratulations from his employer. But he had also been sent written warnings from his manager about poor stock control. After Christmas 1997 H went on holiday and instead of carrying out a detailed stock check he "guesstimated" the stock from his holiday residence in Scotland. On his return to London he was summoned to an investigation at which he admitted guessing the stock figures. This misconduct was interpreted by his manager as falsification of company documents, an offence of gross misconduct liable to summary dismissal and he was dismissed for this and other admitted offences. The employment tribunal found that the decision to dismiss was unfair because the disciplinary inquiry was fatally flawed. Whitbread Plc v Hall [2001]

There is a sample disciplinary procedure in Appendix 3 at the back of the book.

Discipline And The Probationary Period

Many employers require new staff to work a probationary period. It is worth noting that unless the terms of employment specifically state that the disciplinary procedure does *not* apply during the probationary period, they will apply and probationers must therefore be taken through the process.

When the statutory dispute resolution procedures are introduced they will form the minimum standard of performance required of employers. Employees will be entitled to be taken through the disciplinary procedure. Use the statutory minimum during the probationary period then if you have a more sophisticated disciplinary procedure, use that version.

Short Service Disciplinary Procedures

You may have an employee who has successfully passed his probationary period but who still has less than a year's service.

You can include a provision in your disciplinary procedure that staff with short service will be taken through a shorter version of the disciplinary process. In this way, you show that you are the Reasonable Employer by formally warning him and giving him a chance to improve but you can dismiss at an earlier stage than the full procedure allows.

Fairness

The test here is whether you used a fair procedure and whether it was reasonable for you to finally decide to dismiss your employee once the procedure had been carried out.

An employment tribunal would consider some of the following:

❑ Was the employee given a fair hearing?
❑ What evidence was used at the hearing and was it all used?
❑ Did the employee have a representative at the hearing or a trade union official?
❑ If there was more than one employee involved were they all treated in the same way?
❑ Had the employee done this before?
❑ Did you consider warnings? Were these used in the past?
❑ Did you consider the overall performance of the employee. For example, did the employee previously have a long record of good work and behaviour?
❑ Could you have disciplined the employee instead of dismissing him?
❑ Did the employee have an effective right of appeal against the decision?
❑ Was the whole procedure carried out in the same way as previous procedures? If not, how did it differ and why?
❑ Was the conduct of the employee looked into thoroughly?
❑ Did you believe that the employee committed the offence?
❑ Was this belief established after adequate investigation?

You don't need absolute proof in a case of dishonesty, but there must be strong evidence of the dishonesty for you to dismiss an employee.

Who Can Claim Unfair Dismissal?

To qualify for protection against unfair dismissal an employee must meet the following conditions. He must:

❑ Be working full or part-time (the amount of hours worked per week is irrelevant). The self-employed are excluded;
❑ Have one year's continuous employment. See below for exceptions to this rule;
❑ Be below 65 or the normal retirement age for his job at the date of dismissal. There are exceptions to this if the dismissal is based upon discrimination.

The employee has three months from the date of dismissal to bring a claim.

Exceptions To The One Year Rule

There are a number of exceptions to the requirement that an employee must have one year's continuous service. Where the dismissal is for one of the following reasons dismissal will be automatically unfair even where service is less than 12 months:

- ❑ Trade union activities, carried out at an appropriate time. This is usually out of work hours or during work with the employer's permission. (This does not include strikes or working to rule, which are breaches of contract);
- ❑ Belonging to a trade union;
- ❑ Refusing to join a trade union;
- ❑ Where selection for redundancy was connected with a trade union issue;
- ❑ Where dismissal is linked with pregnancy and maternity rights;
- ❑ Shop or betting industry employees who object to working on Sundays;
- ❑ Where an employee is dismissed due to sex, race or disability discrimination;
- ❑ Dismissal relating to an employee asserting their rights under employment laws, for example, taking time off to deal with an emergency involving a dependent;
- ❑ Dismissal of an employee observing health and safety rules;
- ❑ Where an employee is dismissed for acting as an employee representative or was a candidate to become an employee representative;
- ❑ Dismissal relating to an employee asserting his right to be accompanied to a disciplinary or grievance hearing;
- ❑ Dismissal related to an employee acting as a pension scheme trustee;
- ❑ Dismissal relating to the Working Time Regulations;
- ❑ Dismissal relating to an employee asserting his rights under the National Minimum Wage Act 1998;
- ❑ Dismissal relating to an employee participating in protected industrial action;
- ❑ Dismissal relating to an employee asserting his rights under the Tax Credits Act 1999;
- ❑ Dismissal relating to an employee asserting his rights under the Part Time Employees (Prevention of Less Favourable Treatment) Regulations 2000;
- ❑ The selection of an employee for redundancy based upon a reason which would have been automatically unfair if the same reason was used to dismiss the employee.

From October 2004 a failure to follow the statutory discipline and dismissal procedure will be an automatic unfair dismissal. The one year service qualification still applies.

Investigation

If you know (or think you know) that there is a disciplinary problem, you must carry out an investigation to collect, collate and review the relevant facts. The investigation is not part of the formal disciplinary process. Ideally, the investigation should be carried out by someone other than the person likely to chair any disciplinary hearing, although this is not always possible, especially in small firms. It's not a legal requirement to do so.

If a staff member, charged with or convicted of a criminal offence, refuses to co-operate with the investigation, don't be deterred from taking action. He should be advised in writing that unless further information is provided, a disciplinary decision will be taken on the basis of the information available. This could result in dismissal. See investigation checklist on page 35.

You must remember that it is your responsibility as the employer to carry out as much of an investigation as is reasonable in the circumstances. You should have a genuine belief that the employee has committed the act of misconduct, based on reasonable grounds, after a reasonable investigation. The burden of proof in employment law is "a balance of probabilities". The results of the investigation do not have to prove guilt beyond all doubt. The evidence derived from your investigation should persuade a reasonable manager on balance that there are sufficient grounds to take the matter forward to the formal stage and provide sufficient evidence for you to be reasonably sure that the employee did that of which he is accused.

Example: A client, M, discovered that a company petrol card which had been renewed in the name of an employee, L, who had left the company the previous year was being used. The Financial Controller H was responsible for ordering and cancelling cards on behalf of the company. H was unable to explain why the card had been renewed or clarify who was using it. M investigated and the supplier of the petrol cards S send copies of three petrol vouchers. The signature was in L's name, but the style of signature was remarkably similar to H's handwriting, which was very distinctive. H denied that he had used the petrol card. The company asked for a handwriting expert's report. The report showed that the expert found a moderate positive indicator that H had signed the petrol vouchers. In addition, M reviewed all the petrol statements from the time L had left. The pattern of activity mirrored H's arrangements. He had lived in London for some months after L had left the company and at that time the card was regularly used at a London filling station close to where he had lived. When H moved to another area, activity in London stopped and started in the town where H now lived. It stopped altogether when he was on holiday. M carried out searches into the patterns of L's activity before he left the company and concluded that there was no evidence to suggest that he was still unlawfully using the card. M decided that on balance there was adequate proof that H had taken and used the petrol card without authorisation and he was dismissed for gross misconduct.

Investigating Criminal Offences

If an employee is charged with a criminal offence and you believe it is appropriate to take disciplinary action, you should act immediately. For example, you don't need to wait just because the police haven't come to any conclusion with their inquiries. The general principle that disciplinary action should be taken as soon as possible still applies. The burden of proof in civil law is a balance of probabilities. You don't need to prove that the employee was guilty beyond all reasonable doubt which is the burden of proof for a criminal conviction.

Suspension

In cases which appear to involve serious or gross misconduct, you should consider suspension from work whilst the facts are fully investigated. Suspension must not be used for minor infringements. At this stage, suspension should be with full pay. Suspension should be for as short a period of time as is possible as it is a serious step to take.

The sort of situations where you might use suspension would be in cases of:

- Physical violence;
- Harassment (sex, race, disability, religious belief, sexual orientation);
- Fighting;
- Fraud or theft;
- Where the employer genuinely feels that the employee may interfere with the collection of evidence or with witnesses;
- Where the employer believes there is a genuine business risk, for example the suspension of sales or computer staff who could be in a position to cause damage to the organisation.

When suspending staff, you must make it clear that this is just part of the normal investigation process. Don't forget that even staff who are suspended have the right to be accompanied. Arrangements may have to be made for them to meet with their companion in order to prepare their defence.

Suspension should be considered as an option, but should not be an automatic response.

Example: An employee against whom allegations of gross misconduct had been made was suspended on full pay as an automatic response by the employer with no preliminary investigations. The court decided that the employer's hasty action was a breach of contract constituting a breach of the duty of trust and confidence. Gogay v Herts CC [2000]

Checklist Carrying Out An Investigation

There should be a prompt investigation to find out all the relevant facts before memory fades. Include anything the employee wishes to say. If in serious cases there are witnesses, take statements from them at the earliest opportunity. Make sure that the statements are written, dated and signed. Everyone should be clear precisely what the complaint is.

Exactly what you need to do to investigate depends upon the evidence available. For example, if an employee was caught red-handed then the person who caught the employee would be able to give evidence. In other cases it may only be through inference that you have put an allegation of theft to an employee, in which case much more detailed investigation and presentation of evidence to the employee would be required.

When reviewing the situation you must consider all the relevant issues, for example, witness statements, documentary evidence and training records.

❑ What is the employee alleged to have done or failed to do?
❑ What are the circumstances involved? What happened? When did it happen? Who was involved? Where did the incident occur?
❑ What job was being done by the employee? Is it his usual job?
❑ What is the age and length of service of the employee?
❑ How long has the employee been in his present job?
❑ Has the job changed in any way recently?
❑ Has the employee been counselled about his performance before? Was this recorded?
❑ What is the employee's past disciplinary history? Are there any current warnings?
❑ Are there any mitigating circumstances?
❑ Are there any witnesses?
❑ Look at the following documents:
> Training record
> Induction checklist
> Employment contract/ terms/ offer letter
> Job description
❑ Was any injury or damage caused by misconduct?
❑ What normally happens?
❑ Are the standards reasonable and clear? Have they been communicated to the workforce? Can you prove they were aware of the standard required?
❑ Has the employee got an up-to-date copy of the disciplinary procedure?

Preparation For A Disciplinary Hearing

If you do decide that a formal disciplinary hearing is necessary you must give your employee details of the complaint, the procedure to be followed, and advise him that he is required to attend a disciplinary hearing. It's a good idea to write to him, specifying the issues you want to discuss, enclosing copies of any supporting evidence and a copy of your current disciplinary procedure. Allow him sufficient time to prepare his case. The ACAS guidelines suggest five working days, though you can bring this forward by mutual agreement.

You must remind the employee that he has the right to be accompanied by a companion at the hearing. If the employee belongs to a union which is not recognised by the company, and he wants his companion to be an external union representative make sure you ask for confirmation that the representative is a suitable person and ask to see his union card as identification. The employee may offer a reasonable alternative date if his chosen companion cannot attend.

Collate all the relevant material. This may include personal details, disciplinary record, any current warnings, other relevant documents (for instance clock cards, absence or sickness records) and, where appropriate, written statements from witnesses.

Be careful when dealing with evidence from an informant who wishes to remain anonymous. This doesn't necessarily cast their evidence into doubt, but you should look for evidence to support it. Check that the informant's motives are genuine.

Explore whether the standards of other staff are acceptable, or whether this person is being unfairly singled out. Think through what explanations may be offered, and if possible check them out beforehand. Think about the structure of the hearing and make a list of points you will want to cover and questions you wish to ask.

Arrange a time for the hearing, which should be held as privately as possible, in a suitable room, and where there will be no interruptions.

Try to have a second member of management to take notes of the proceedings and who can act as a witness if necessary. Even when you're fairly experienced it's really difficult for one person to chair a disciplinary meeting, ask questions, listen to answers and make full notes. Never go in alone where your employee is accompanied.

Where possible ensure that any witnesses who can do so attend the hearing, unless the employee accepts in advance that the witness statements are statements of fact. If the witness is from outside the organisation and is not prepared or is unable to attend the hearing, try and get a written statement.

If you think there may be problems with understanding or language consider the provision of an interpreter (perhaps a friend of the employee, or a fellow employee).

Note Taking

I cannot sufficiently emphasise the importance of taking clear accurate notes at the disciplinary hearing. They'll be important if the decision is appealed internally, and vital if your employee is dismissed and brings a claim for unfair dismissal. The notes should accurately reflect your employee's explanation and any admissions he might make, the questions put and his responses. They should also create a record of the formalities of the hearing so that there is no doubt that he was advised of all the important issues.

Your records should give details of the nature of any breach of disciplinary rules or unsatisfactory performance, the defence or mitigation put forward, the action taken and the reasons for it, whether an appeal was lodged, its outcome and any subsequent developments. These records should be kept confidential and retained in accordance with the disciplinary procedure and the Data Protection Act 1998, which requires the release of certain data to individuals on their request. Copies of any meeting records should be given to your employee if he requests it, although, in certain circumstances, some information may be withheld, for example, to protect a witness.

Before the meeting ends I usually ask the employee to read my notes of the disciplinary hearing and sign and date each page indicating agreement that the notes are a true representation of the discussion. That way we avoid later disputes about what was or wasn't said.

It's OK to use tape recording as a recording method if the method has been agreed by both parties in advance, but you do need to make sure that the recording equipment is capable of doing the job required and doesn't run out half way through the hearing.

Stages Of The Disciplinary Process

Informal v Formal

When dealing with a disciplinary matter it is vital for all concerned to be clear about the status of the meeting. There are a number of key differences between an informal discussion, often referred to as "counselling" or a "chat" and a formal meeting.

You should prepare for both types of meeting even though the status is different.

Informal Advice

The nature and seriousness of the offence in question will dictate your response. In the case of fairly minor misconduct, such as timekeeping, you should adopt an informal counselling approach before using the formal warning route.

Plunging into formal warnings too early or giving an unduly harsh warning may be counter-productive and in one recent case was even found to be constructive dismissal.

Main Differences Between Informal and Formal Discussions

Informal	Formal
No right to be accompanied	Right to be accompanied offered
No notice of meeting	Advance notice
No prior information provided	Outline of the reason for meeting
Diary note kept in the supervisor's file	Documented confirmation of any warning, copy kept on personal file
No formal warning only advice to help employee improve	Disciplinary penalty may be imposed
No appeal process	Appeal must be offered
No set duration or review period	Warnings lapse after set time
Manager/ supervisor handles alone	Minute taker or another manager present
Only for minor offences	More serious offences or failure to respond to informal approach

Example: S had worked for her employer for five years and had never been given any formal warnings. One day she had a heated discussion with a colleague. She felt so drained and upset that she left the office for 90 minutes. She was entitled to a 30 minute lunch break. On her return her supervisor saw that she was still very upset and sent her home. The company disciplined her for her unauthorised absence and issued a final written warning. S resigned claiming constructive dismissal. The court agreed with S that the penalty was unduly onerous in this case. Stanley Cole(Wainfleet) Ltd v Sheriden [2003]

N.B. It is not appropriate to hold a counselling session with an employee who has committed a serious conduct offence such as fighting.

Holding A Disciplinary Hearing

A disciplinary hearing should be conducted in a structured way, with you as chairperson clearly guiding participants through the process, but allowing for a two-way exchange of information.

Always get there early and set out the meeting room appropriately for a formal meeting. Once the hearing starts, introduce those present and explain their roles. State the purpose of the hearing and explain how it will be conducted. Ask the employee if he has had enough time to prepare and if he understands why you are having the hearing. It's useful to have this on record.

When you outline the case state precisely what the complaint is and go through the evidence that has been gathered. The employee and his companion should be allowed to see any statements made by witnesses.

The point of the hearing is to discover the truth, not catch people out. It should be an exploration of the facts. Find out whether the employee is prepared to accept that he may have done something wrong. If so, you can agree the steps which should be taken to remedy the situation.

Allow the employee to state his case and answer any allegations which have been made. He should be able to ask questions, put forward his side of events and call witnesses. The companion may also ask questions and confer privately with the employee, but is not allowed to answer on his behalf. Listen carefully and be prepared to wait in silence for an answer as this can encourage the employee to be more forthcoming.

Ask questions to establish all the facts. Ask open-ended questions, for example, 'what happened then?' to get the broad picture. Ask precise, closed questions requiring a yes/no answer only when specific information is needed. When you've asked a question, stop and wait for the reply – don't answer it yourself! This happens quite often especially in cases where the employee doesn't reply immediately. Inexperienced managers tend to give a sort of multiple choice of possible answers. For example a manger might say something along these lines:

"Why were you late on the dates I mentioned?" (no reply from employee)
"Was it because the bus was late?" (still no reply) *".... or the baby's teething and kept you awake all night so you overslept?"* (silence) *".... or there were road works on that road and you were delayed?"*

You get the general picture.......

If in the course of the hearing, either during the employee's explanation or later on, details emerge which require further investigation, adjourn the hearing.

Make sure that the companion is offered the opportunity to contribute. In some cases it may be difficult to restrain the companion whose strategy may be to talk as much as possible. This tactic minimises the opportunities for the employee to speak. You may find that you end up discussing all sorts of matters which will probably be quite irrelevant to the issue under consideration. Politely silence the companion and direct everyone's attention back to the key issues under discussion. Remind the companion of his role and reiterate that you need to hear his version of events from your employee's own mouth.

If it has become clear during the hearing that the employee has provided an adequate explanation or there is no real evidence to support the allegation, stop the proceedings, tell him that you are satisfied with his explanation and you will not be taking any further action.

Disciplinary hearings can be quite stressful for all concerned, but try to maintain a calm and polite approach. Don't get involved in arguments or make personal or humiliating remarks. Avoid physical contact or gestures which could be misinterpreted or misconstrued as judgemental.

If your employee becomes upset or distressed during the hearing allow time for him to regain his composure before continuing. You may have to adjourn for a while to allow him to recover his poise. This doesn't mean that he's off the hook, but that the meeting will be reconvened later on. Sometimes during the course of the hearing there are frank exchanges. Don't let abusive language or conduct which could be construed as gross misconduct pass without comment. If necessary this itself must be dealt with on a disciplinary basis. Adjourn this hearing and convene a later one, where both issues can be considered together. Consider suspending your employee with pay to enable him to calm down and to allow a full investigation.

If a grievance is raised during the hearing about the way in which you have handled the case, or the way in which it was investigated, ACAS recommend that you suspend the disciplinary procedure for a short period until the grievance can be considered. It may also be appropriate to bring another manager in to deal with the disciplinary case.

Once everyone has given their views, summarise the main points of the discussion. This allows all parties to be reminded of the nature of the offence, the arguments and evidence put forward and to ensure nothing is missed. Ask your employee if he feels that he has had a fair hearing, and whether he has anything further to say.

Always – *always*! - adjourn before making a decision, even in the most clear-cut case. If you produce a document confirming a disciplinary penalty at that stage, it looks very much as though the decision was a foregone conclusion. An adjournment will help you come to a clear view about the facts. It is also important to ensure that you are seen to have acted fairly.

If the facts are disputed, you have to decide on the balance of probability which version of events is true. A balance of probabilities doesn't mean that you have to have proof beyond reasonable doubt. All it means is that on balance the reasonable manager would reach the conclusion you did.

Before deciding on any disciplinary penalty consider:

❑ The seriousness of the offence, and whether the procedure gives guidance;
❑ The penalty imposed in similar cases in the past;
❑ The individual's disciplinary record and general service;
❑ Any mitigating circumstances;
❑ Whether the proposed penalty is reasonable in all the circumstances;
❑ Any current warnings for related offences.

Once you have had a chance to consider the outcome, reconvene the disciplinary hearing. Clearly inform the employee of your decision and the penalty, if any. If you have issued a warning explain what improvement is expected, how long the warning will last, and what the consequences of failure to improve may be. Explain the right of appeal and how it operates

You must keep a record of what action you have decided upon. Where you have agreed an action plan or issued a formal warning, you should confirm these to the individual in writing.

A checklist of all the disciplinary hearing key points is included on page 43.

Disciplinary Penalties

Nobody should be dismissed for a first offence, unless it's an offence which constitutes gross misconduct. Gross misconduct should be identified and listed in your disciplinary procedure.

Tell the employee verbally of your decision (even if your decision is to take no further action) and follow it up in writing.

Your employee should be in no doubt about what action is being taken under the disciplinary procedure. He must also be very clear about what he has to do to avoid further disciplinary action, and by when. Your letter should include:

- What was included in the discussions;
- Any agreements or admissions;
- The disciplinary penalty, if any, and its duration;
- The reason for the decision;
- The actions being taken as a result of that decision;
- The specific improvement required of the employee;
- Review period;
- The right to appeal.

It is not enough to make comments such as "you must improve your attendance". Be very specific in your requirements. Any warning letter must state clearly how much improvement you want to see and what standard of performance is required together with an indication of the timescale that will be given for the improvement to take place.

Being Specific About Improvements

I have said that the purpose of discipline is improvement. Generalities don't work; you must specify exactly what improvements you expect to see. If you say that you're only making 35 widgets an hour and everyone else is making 50 widgets an hour and we need an improvement, don't be surprised if the widget making increases to 37 an hour. You've got what you asked for but not what you wanted. There are different ways of specifying what's needed and some examples are shown below:

- Percentages or ratios - e.g. 'Your current absence rate is 22%, the company target is 8%';
- Frequency of occurrence - e.g. 'You are to hold a weekly team meeting in order to improve communication in your section';
- Averages - e.g. 'You must achieve an average of 75% of monthly sales target within three months. This will be reviewed on a monthly basis for the duration of this warning';
- Time - e.g. 'You must respond to callouts within one hour in future';
- Zero tolerance - e.g. 'Any further conduct of this nature will result in further disciplinary action being taken';
- Company standard - e.g. 'You must achieve the sales target set and agreed at national levels'.

The main thing is to remember to monitor your employee's performance during the warning period. It is important not to forget about it. He is entitled to be given regular feedback on his progress towards the expected standards. Hold regular review meetings to discuss his performance and take feedback from him. Keep records of your discussions. If there is no improvement within a reasonable time, such meetings may also remind you to trigger an escalation of the matter to the next stage of the disciplinary process.

Formal Warnings

Most employers adopt a three stage warning approach:

- Verbal warning, often for six months;
- First written warning, often for twelve months;
- Final written warning, often for twelve months.

Some small employers will reduce the number of warnings. The law does not lay down the length of time during which warnings will remain live. That's the choice of the individual organisation, but it is subject to the over-riding requirement of reasonableness.

You need to clearly explain what the warning means, how long it will remain live on the file and what will happen if there is a repetition of the offence (or any other offence).

You should make a diary note of the expiry date of each warning. Once a warning has expired, the general rule is that you have to start from square one again.

Put a copy of formal warnings on your employee's personal file. If the warning expires without further action being necessary, it can be removed from the file, although a note should always be kept that the warning was issued for [offence] on [date], removed on [date] and no further action was necessary.

Checklist Disciplinary Hearing

To ensure that any disciplinary interview is carried out effectively and fairly it is essential to take the following actions:

- ❑ Consider all the facts of the case.
- ❑ Tell the employee about the complaint made against him.
- ❑ Explain the procedure you are following and inform the employee that he may be required to attend a disciplinary interview.
- ❑ If the investigation confirms that action needs to be taken, notify your employee, agree the date of the next meeting and inform him of his right to be accompanied.
- ❑ Check all the prevailing circumstances affecting a situation – personal difficulties for example.
- ❑ Check all the evidence submitted by others. Be particularly wary of anonymous complaints. Take all witness statements well in advance.
- ❑ Ensure that this individual is not being singled out. Is his performance/ conduct measurably worse than others who are not subject to discipline?
- ❑ Hold the interview and give your employee every opportunity to explain matters.
- ❑ Take time to check the explanations where possible. Have documentation and witnesses available.
- ❑ Give the employee ample time to prepare a response to the allegations. ACAS recommend up to five working days.
- ❑ Involve full time union officials whenever disciplinary action involves trade union representatives.
- ❑ Ensure that disciplinary interviews are carried out at a location which is suitable for the purpose and free from interruptions.
- ❑ Make sure that all relevant information is available at the meeting.
- ❑ Do not be bound by precedent but be aware of the types of disciplinary action taken in the past in similar circumstances.
- ❑ Never conduct disciplinary hearings alone – arrange to be accompanied by someone capable of acting as a witness and taking notes.
- ❑ Conduct the interview in a calm structured way, making notes of the points to be covered.
- ❑ At the end of the meeting summarise the main points. Investigate any areas that need to be checked.
- ❑ Do not hesitate to adjourn during the hearing to check information.
- ❑ It is sensible to take your time at the end of the meeting to review your decision. A hasty announcement of any disciplinary penalty makes it look as though it was pre-determined. ·
- ❑ Always inform the employee of the outcome including:
- - the reason for the decision;
- - the action being taken;
- - the specific improvement required of the employee;
- - the time-scale in which the improvement must take place;
- - the duration of any warning;
- - how the improvement is to be measured.
- ❑ Confirmation of disciplinary penalties must be given in writing to the employee.
- ❑ Ensure that the employee is given full details of how to lodge an appeal against the decision.
- ❑ An explanation must be given of the next stage of the proceedings if there is a failure to improve.

The Data Protection Act gives employees the right to see disciplinary notes held on their personal file, though they will not be automatically entitled to access third party witness statements if to do so would reveal the identity of the witness. The witness would have to give permission.

A checklist is shown below followed by two sample letters.

Checklist Formal Warning Letters

Items to be included in formal warning letters are as follows:

- ❏ Ensure the warning letter is dated. Specify the start date of the warning period;
- ❏ The warning letter should refer to the disciplinary hearing. Clarify whether the employee was accompanied, and if so, by whom. If the employee opted to be unaccompanied, include this in the letter;
- ❏ Warning letters must contain clear instructions as to the action required by the individual in order to meet the standards that the company requires;
- ❏ It is important to point out to the employee what stage has been reached in the disciplinary process;
- ❏ Warning letters should contain clear guidance as to what happens next if the employee fails to attain the standards of performance or conduct required within the stated time period;
- ❏ It is good practice for warning letters to refer to the company's own disciplinary rules and procedures. Wordings similar to 'in accordance with the company's disciplinary procedure we consider this to be a serious breach of conduct, and as the procedure indicates, this results in the issue of a formal written warning';
- ❏ It is vital that warning letters state clearly how long the warning is to last. The letter should also indicate that the performance or conduct will be reviewed at regular intervals during the warning period;
- ❏ Warning letters must refer to an appeal procedure. This is an important issue. Warning letters must contain an outline of the right of appeal, stating to whom the appeal should be made, and by when. It's a good idea to ask the employee to confirm the reason for the appeal;
- ❏ A copy of any warning letter must be placed on the employee's personal file.

Sample first written warning to employee

Dear

First written warning

I write to confirm the points made to you at our disciplinary meeting on [ ], at which you were represented by [   ]. The meeting was held to discuss your conduct on the previous Saturday morning, 10 May. On Friday 9 May, you agreed to work overtime on the following day as an urgent job was required by an important customer. Based on your promise to work overtime, the customer was informed that the job would be ready for collection at midday, Saturday. You were aware of this commitment to the customer.

You did not turn up for work on the Saturday morning. No contact was made with your supervisor or manager as required in cases of absence. As a result, a key customer was let down. When asked for an explanation, you said that you 'must have overslept after visiting friends on the Friday evening and having a few drinks'.

At the disciplinary hearing you were informed that this was considered as serious misconduct. In accordance with the company disciplinary procedure, of which you have a copy, serious misconduct of this nature entitles us to miss a stage in the disciplinary process. Accordingly, the decision at the hearing was to issue you with a written warning, which is stage II of the procedure. Again, in accordance with the procedure this warning will remain in force for 12 months from the date of this letter, expiring on [date].

The next time you agree to work overtime and complete a task for a customer, you will be expected to do so. If for any reason you cannot, you must contact your supervisor or manager as soon as possible so that alternative arrangements can be made to complete the customer order. A failure to do this, will result in a final written warning.

You have the right to appeal against this written warning. If you wish to do so, please write to [name] by [date], stating the reason for your appeal.

Please sign and return the attached copy of this warning. This will be placed on your personal file.

Yours sincerely

Sample final written warning to employee

Dear

I write to confirm the points made at our meeting on [   ].

As you are aware, over the past [   ] months you have failed to meet the standards required by this company in the following respects: **[list areas in which performance or conduct has fallen below the required standards]**.

As discussed with you, we have agreed to give you until [insert date] to meet the required standard. This means that you will need to take the following actions: **[list actions to be taken to meet the required standard of performance]**.

I must warn you that, in view of the previous warnings you have been given, if you fail to achieve the standard of performance/conduct **[delete as appropriate]** required by the company by the above date, you will be dismissed.

You have the right to appeal to **[name]** by **[date]**. If you wish to lodge an appeal you should do so in writing giving the reasons for your appeal.

Please sign and return the enclosed copy of this final written warning as acknowledgement of receipt.

Yours sincerely

How Do Penalties Apply?

Disciplinary procedures tend to follow one of two routes for penalties.

Three Strikes And You're Out

In this scenario, disciplinary penalties awarded while there is another warning live on the record will replace the original penalty and run from that date. The disciplinary procedure must clearly state that once a disciplinary penalty has been awarded, a further breach of either the same, *or any other* unrelated offence (i.e. another conduct matter if the original warning is for a conduct matter), will allow you to escalate the matter to the next stage of the disciplinary process.

Example: J's time-keeping is poor. He receives a formal verbal warning, which in our case remains live for six months.

During the six months his time-keeping is fine, but his manager finds him making a call to his girlfriend in Australia. This is an unauthorised use of company equipment. J is taken through the disciplinary procedure and given a first written warning. The verbal warning disappears, the first written warning remains. This will be live for 12 months.

During the next 12 months J refuses to wear his company uniform on several occasions. He receives a final written warning and the first written warning is removed from the file. The final written warning remains live on the file for 12 months.

If there is another conduct breach within the next 12 months, J will be dismissed because these are all conduct matters, although different in nature.

N.B. If at this stage J's performance suffers, it would be unfair to dismiss for a breach under the capability heading, because all his other warnings are for conduct. The two should not be mixed. J gets a warning for capability and keeps the separate conduct warning too.

Generic Grouping

In some companies, warnings will only be escalated to the next stage if the employee repeats his breach of the same rule or standard while the first warning is live on the file. It means that an employee can have a substantial number of warnings on his file at any one time, all at different stages.

Example: J's time-keeping is poor. He receives a verbal warning, which remains live for six months.

During the six months his time-keeping is fine, but his manager finds him making a call to his girlfriend in Australia. This is an unauthorised use of company equipment. J is taken through the disciplinary procedure and given another verbal warning for breach of a different rule. The first verbal warning remains.

During the next six months J refuses to wear his company uniform on several occasions. He receives another verbal warning (breach for yet another reason) and the first verbal warning is removed from the file as there's been no repeat during the six months it was live of his time-keeping problems.

Demotion

Some procedures allow an employer to demote an employee. This will normally be used in the capability process where the employee has had several warnings, but has failed to improve to meet the standard.

It should not normally be used as a means of punishment. If you demote an employee inappropriately or without the sanction of the disciplinary process, the employee may be able to resign and claim constructive dismissal.

Example: H worked at a builders yard for twenty years, serving customers and dealing with cash transactions. He had no written job description. The employers were concerned that customers had left the yard without a sales invoice. H explained this by saying he was striking a balance between building materials bought by the yard and the value of the purchases made. SBM were not satisfied with his explanation, thought he had acted dishonestly and decided to transfer him to other work not involving cash. He was told he was 'not suitable to be employed in a position of trust'. No disciplinary procedure was followed. When H was sent a letter setting out his new role he resigned and claimed unfair dismissal. The EAT said that 'Requiring an employee to cease doing what had been his principal job, and to require him to take up a new role, in circumstances in which there had been no allegations of dishonesty, would in our view amount to a variation of the employee's contract'. Further they did not think such a variation could be imposed without consent. Hilton v Shiner Builders Merchants [2001]

Dismissal

Dismissal is the ultimate sanction. This last step should only be taken if, despite warnings, conduct or performance has not improved over the required time period. Unless the case involves gross misconduct, the employee should be issued with a final warning before dismissal takes place.

All dismissals, except those for gross misconduct, will be with notice. The statutory minimum notice periods are shown in this table

Statutory Notice Periods

0-4 weeks	No notice required
4 weeks – 2 years	One week
2-12 years	One additional week for each completed year of service to maximum of 12 weeks at 12 years or more service

Notice periods can be extended by contract.

If your contract allows for it, payment in lieu may be given for the notice period. The calculation of payment in lieu of notice should include the value of any contractual benefits such as the use of a company car.

If you don't have a clause in your contract which allows you to make payment in lieu of giving notice, then paying notice in lieu will be a wrongful dismissal i.e. dismissal in breach of contract.

Summary Dismissal

Summary dismissal is dismissal without notice or pay in lieu following an act of gross misconduct. These are determined by the company and you should list acts which constitute gross misconduct in your disciplinary procedure. In many companies failure to wear company uniform properly or at all is a fairly minor matter. In haulage company Eddie Stobart's rule-book, failure to wear a tie is gross misconduct. Gross misconduct is an act which constitutes a fundamental breach of contract by the employee. As a result you may dismiss him without notice, but you must still follow all the usual disciplinary procedures (remember Whitbread v Hall). The employee is entitled to his pay to the date of the dismissal and any holiday accrued but not taken. If your contract contains a clause that allows the company to withhold holiday pay in the event of a dismissal for gross misconduct, you will only be able to withhold holiday which exceeds the statutory minimum (four weeks).

Example: *M worked for W as a steward. He had a term in his contract that, if he was dismissed on grounds of dishonesty, then the amount of pay for holiday accrued but not taken would be nil. M was dismissed having admitted taking money from his employers and at the time of the dismissal had accrued 26 days' holiday. W refused to pay this, and M brought a claim in the employment tribunal. The Working Time Regulations (WTR) state that an employee is entitled to be paid in lieu of annual leave accrued but not taken at the time his employment ends. The court decided that an agreement not to pay the minimum statutory annual leave accrued under the WTR on the termination of an employee's contract of employment will be void. Witley & District Mens' Club v Mackay [2001]*

Instant Dismissal

If you dismiss a member of staff without going through the formal disciplinary process it will be an unfair dismissal. Even where an employee is caught red-handed and admits his misdemeanours, a dismissal which takes place without holding a full disciplinary hearing, is likely to be unfair.

Constructive Dismissal

This is where the employee leaves his job as a result of his employer's behaviour. For example, the employer has made the employee's life very difficult and the employee feels that he cannot remain in his job. An employee can resign over one serious incident or over a build up of a number of incidents. However, he must resign soon after the incident in order to be able to rely upon it. The employer's actions must have amounted to a *fundamental* breach of contract. An employee being constructively dismissed only proves that he was dismissed, it does not automatically prove that the dismissal was unfair. He then has to prove that the dismissal was also unfair.

Examples of constructive dismissal can include:

❑ Not supporting managers in difficult work situations;
❑ Harassing or humiliating staff, particularly in front of other less senior staff, clients or the public;
❑ Victimising or targeting particular members of staff;
❑ Changing the employee's job content or terms without consultation;
❑ Making a significant change in the employee's job location at short notice;
❑ Falsely accusing an employee of misconduct such as theft or of being incapable of carrying out his job;
❑ Excessive demotion or disciplining of employees;
❑ Refusal of a pay rise to one employee when everyone else got one.

To establish constructive dismissal, the employee must show that four conditions have been met:

❑ The employer has fundamentally breached the contract, or there is an intention on the employer's part no longer to be bound by an essential term of the contract;
❑ That the employer's breach caused the employee to leave;
❑ That the employee did not act too soon by leaving before the breach took place; and
❑ That the employee did not waive the right to terminate the contract after the breach took place by delaying too long before resigning.

There are no specific rules about what constitutes a fundamental breach of contract. It is for the court or employment tribunal to determine whether such a breach has occurred, depending on the facts of the situation and the impact on the individual.

Pitfalls For The Unwary

Employee's Failure To Attend The Disciplinary Hearing

Sometimes employees fail to attend a disciplinary hearing. There has been a noticeable trend recently for employees facing the disciplinary process to go sick with stress. If your employee doesn't attend the hearing either through sickness or for some other reason, write to him rescheduling the date for the meeting. Ask him to confirm his attendance. If he fails to attend the next meeting, write again rescheduling the meeting. This time add that if he fails to attend on the third occasion you will proceed in his absence. Remind him that if he is unable to attend himself you will accept written representations from him or he may send his companion to speak on his behalf.

If he fails to attend without good reason on the third occasion, hold the disciplinary hearing in his absence and work with the information that you have available to you. Write to the employee informing him of your decision and offer an appeal where a disciplinary penalty has been imposed.

Resignations Before The Disciplinary Hearing

It often happens that a manager who is about to take an employee through the disciplinary process, suggests that the employee should resign rather than face dismissal. This may be very well intentioned, for example, to save the employee the embarrassment of being dismissed. Don't do it. Your job is to apply the disciplinary procedure. To circumvent it, even if it's for the best of reasons, can lead you to a constructive dismissal claim.

If an employee resigns of his own volition rather than face the disciplinary process, he is entitled to do so.

Resignations During The Disciplinary Hearing

Occasionally an employee going through the hearing will conclude that he's likely to be dismissed and will ask to resign. Adopt the Magnus Magnusson approach ("I've started so I'll finish.") and complete the hearing process.

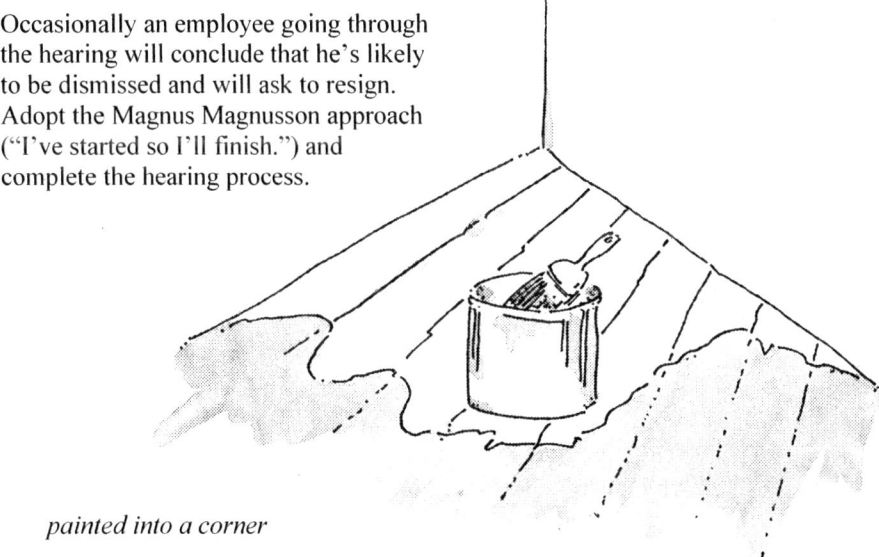

painted into a corner

The risk here is that if you allow a resignation in these circumstances, the employee may claim duress later and thus constructive dismissal. The risk is increased if you are chairing the meeting by yourself.

Custom And Practice

Some terms and conditions of employment become established because they have become an accepted way of doing things for some time. They are often not written down but are widely adopted and can form part of the employment contract.

For a term to be regarded as 'custom and practice', it must be:

- Reasonable - it must be approved by a court or tribunal;
- Certain - it must be able to be defined precisely;
- Notorious - it must be long-established and well known;
- Not inconsistent with an express term or some other implied term of the contract;
- Necessary to give business efficacy to the performance of the contract.

Custom and practice is usually associated with matters like the custom of early finishing on Fridays, but it can arise in discipline too.

Example: A Christian charitable housing association always tried to give their staff one last chance when applying the disciplinary process. Over the years they had formed the habit of giving not just a Final Written Warning, which was part of the disciplinary procedure, but a Final, Final Written Warning, which was not.

A new manager arrived at one site and eventually dismissed a black woman, B, who at that stage was on a Final Written Warning. The manager was not aware of the practice of issuing Final Final Written Warnings. B claimed that she'd been unlawfully discriminated against on grounds of her colour because she was treated less favourably than her white colleagues. The case was settled out of court with the association accepting liability and making appropriate compensation.

How Many Final Warnings?

You would think that a final warning would mean just that – one warning and the next step is dismissal. Many companies fall into the trap of giving repeat final written warnings. This tends to happen when they are short staffed and feel that they can't afford to lose people. It doesn't work as a strategy (that staff member is still failing to meet your standards) and everyone else becomes complacent about the way you apply your process. If your procedure works on the Three Strikes basis and you keep giving final warnings, at what point do you dismiss? How can an employee with five written warnings distinguish between five and six final written warnings? He may be able to argue that he was unfairly dismissed because he's had all these final written warnings and never been dismissed. What's different this time? It's a fair comment.

Always stick to your procedure, unless there are genuine mitigating circumstances.

Section 6   Appeals

The opportunity to appeal against a disciplinary decision is essential to natural justice. The ACAS Code recommends that you provide an opportunity to appeal against a formal disciplinary penalty up to and including dismissal. Appeals may be raised for various reasons, for example, the discovery of new evidence, undue harshness or inconsistency of the penalty. It is also an opportunity to correct defects in the original disciplinary procedure. N.B. It is *not* good practice to increase the penalty on appeal.

Appeals Procedure

A good appeals procedure should:

- Specify a time within which the appeal should be lodged. The ACAS code recommends five working days;
- Provide for appeals to be dealt with quickly;
- Advise of the right to be accompanied at the appeal hearing;
- Provide for the appeal to be heard by someone senior in authority to the person who took the disciplinary decision. If possible, whoever hears the appeal should not have been involved at the earlier stage;
- Specify what action may be taken by those hearing the appeal;
- Allow the employee, or his representative the opportunity to comment on any new evidence arising during the appeal before any decision is taken.

Small firms often find it difficult to identify someone with higher authority than the person who took the original disciplinary decision to hear the appeal. In this case your disciplinary procedure can provide for an independent third party to be nominated.

Hearing An Appeal

Beforehand ensure that:

- Your employee knows when and where it is to be held;
- He is aware of his right to be accompanied;
- The relevant records and notes of the original hearing are available.

At the hearing:

- Introduce those present to each other, explaining their function;
- Explain the purpose of the hearing, how it will be conducted, and the powers held by the person hearing the appeal;

- ❏ Ask the staff member why he is appealing against the disciplinary penalty;
- ❏ Listen carefully to any new evidence that has been introduced. Give the staff member the opportunity to comment;
- ❏ Once the relevant issues have been thoroughly explored, summarise the facts and adjourn to consider the decision;
- ❏ You should not be afraid to overturn a previous decision if it becomes apparent that it was not soundly based;
- ❏ Inform your employee of the results of the appeal and the reasons for the decision and confirm it in writing. Make it clear, if this is the case, that this decision is final.

Discipline: Summary Of Key Points

- ❏ Handle the matter promptly but don't rush into things;
- ❏ Gather all the relevant facts;
- ❏ Collect witness statements at the earliest opportunity, ensuring that the statements are written, dated and signed;
- ❏ Consider suspension with pay whilst the case is being investigated if it is appropriate;
- ❏ Remain objective, fair and above all act consistently;
- ❏ Consider each case on its merits;
- ❏ Don't make snap decisions in the heat of the moment;
- ❏ Follow the organisation's disciplinary procedures;
- ❏ Advise the employee of the disciplinary outcome, preferably in writing;
- ❏ Offer the employee an appeal against any disciplinary action taken.

Section 7   Bullying and Harassment

We hear of so many instances of workplace bullying and harassment that we thought it worth covering the subject here. It is your duty as the Reasonable Employer to identify and root out bullying and harassing behaviour.

Everyone should be treated with dignity and respect at work. Bullying and harassment of any kind are in no-one's interest and you should make sure that they are not tolerated in the workplace. It's a common misconception that only women suffer sexual harassment, but anyone can suffer and it's extremely upsetting.

Example: At a training course the group was discussing harassment and how distressing it can be. I asked if anyone had ever suffered harassment at work. One man C said that he had. He said that he had been a van driver's mate when he first left school, delivering clean uniforms into food factories.
In one factory most of the shop floor were women in their late 30s and early 40s. He said they made his life an absolute misery with their comments, jokes and remarks about what they'd like to do to him. He said while they never actually laid hands on him, they frightened him to the point that he couldn't face going in there any more and after six weeks he left his job. C was quite a big man and assertive in his

bullying and harassment are unacceptable

manner. You would think he'd be well able to look after himself, but he confessed that the sexual harassment drove him out of his job.

As an employer you face legal risks arising from the following categories:

❑   Constructive dismissal
❑   Personal injury
❑   Health and safety
❑   Discrimination

For practical purposes those making a complaint usually define what they mean by bullying or harassment as something which has happened to them that is unwelcome, unwarranted and has a detrimental effect. If employees complain they are being bullied or harassed, then they have a grievance which must be dealt with regardless of whether or not their complaint accords with a standard definition.

Bullying may be characterised as offensive, intimidating, malicious or insulting behaviour, an abuse or misuse of power through means intended to undermine, humiliate, denigrate or injure the recipient.

Harassment, in general terms, is unwanted conduct affecting the dignity of men and women in the workplace. It may be related to age, sex, race, disability, religion, nationality or any personal characteristic of the individual, and may be persistent or an isolated incident. The key is that the actions or comments are viewed as demeaning and unacceptable to the recipient.

It's not always easy to define what's meant by bullying or harassment. What is bullying in one person's eyes, may be considered firm management by another. Most people will agree on extreme cases of bullying and harassment but it is sometimes the grey areas that cause most problems. It's a good idea to give examples of what is unacceptable behaviour in your organization. This may include:

❑ Spreading malicious rumours, or insulting someone (particularly on the grounds of race, sex, sexual orientation and religion or belief);
❑ Copying memos that are critical about someone to others who do not need to know;
❑ Ridiculing or demeaning someone — picking on them or setting them up to fail;
❑ Exclusion or victimisation;
❑ Unfair treatment;
❑ Overbearing supervision or other misuse of power or position;
❑ Unwelcome sexual advances — touching, standing too close, display of offensive materials;
❑ Making threats or comments about job security without foundation;
❑ Deliberately undermining a competent employee by overloading and constant criticism;
❑ Preventing individuals progressing by intentionally blocking promotion or training opportunities.

Bullying and harassment are not necessarily carried out on a face to face basis. It may be by written communications, e-mail ('flame-mail'), text or phone.

People being bullied or harassed may sometimes appear to overreact to something that seems relatively trivial but which may be the last straw following a series of incidents. There is often fear of retribution if they do make a complaint. Colleagues may be reluctant to come forward as witnesses, as they too may fear the consequences for themselves. They may be so relieved not to be the subject of the bully themselves that they collude with the bully as a way of avoiding attention.

Why Should You Care?

Bullying and harassment are not only unacceptable on moral grounds but may, if unchecked or badly handled, create serious problems for an organisation including:

❑ Poor morale and poor employee relations;
❑ Loss of respect for managers and supervisors ;

- Poor performance;
- Lost productivity;
- Absence;
- Resignations;
- Damage to company reputation;
- Tribunal and other court cases and payment of unlimited compensation.

What Should You Do?

First, consider developing a formal policy. This need not be over-elaborate, especially for small firms, and might be included in other personnel policies, but a checklist for a specific policy on bullying and harassment could include the following:

- Statement of commitment from senior management;
- A clear statement that bullying and harassment will not be tolerated;
- Examples of unacceptable behaviour;
- A statement that bullying and harassment may be treated as disciplinary offences;
- The steps the organisation takes to prevent bullying and harassment;
- Responsibilities of supervisors and managers;
- Confidentiality for any complainant;
- Reference to grievance procedures (formal and informal), including timescales for action;
- Investigation procedures, including timescales for action;
- Reference to disciplinary procedures, including timescales for action counselling and support availability;
- Training for managers;
- Protection from victimisation;
- How the policy is to be implemented, reviewed and monitored.

It should be made clear that the policy applies to staff on and off the premises, including those working away from base. The policy should also make plain that bullying or harassment of staff by visitors to the organisation or other third parties will not be tolerated.

All organisations, large and small, should have policies and procedures for dealing with grievance and disciplinary matters. Staff should know to whom they can turn if they have a work-related problem, and managers should be trained in all aspects of the organisation's policies in this sensitive area.

Set a good example. The behaviour of employers and senior managers is as important as any formal policy. Strong management can unfortunately sometimes tip over into bullying behaviour. A culture where employees are consulted and problems discussed is less likely to encourage bullying and harassment than one where there is an authoritarian management style. The organisation must make it clear that bullying and harassment are unacceptable.

Establish fair procedures for dealing promptly with complaints from employees. Complaints of bullying and harassment can usually be dealt with using clear grievance and disciplinary procedures. Such procedures should have provision for confidentiality, and for both the person bringing the complaint and the subject of the complaint to be accompanied by a fellow employee or trade union representative of their choice.

Set standards of behaviour. An organisational statement to all staff about the standards of behaviour expected can make it easier for staff to be fully aware of their responsibilities to others.

This may include information about what constitutes bullying and harassment. Many organisations find it helpful to supplement basic information with guidance booklets and training sessions or seminars. Training can increase awareness of the damage bullying and harassment does both to the organisation and to the individual.

Let employees know that complaints of bullying and/or harassment, or information from staff relating to such complaints, will be dealt with fairly, confidentially and sensitively. Employees will be reluctant to come forward if they feel they may be treated unsympathetically or are likely to be confronted aggressively by the person whose behaviour they are complaining about.

How Should You Respond To A Complaint?

Investigate the complaint promptly, fairly and objectively. Take the complaint seriously. Employees don't normally make serious accusations unless they feel extremely aggrieved. Decisions can then be made as to what action needs to be taken.

- Don't trivialise or make assumptions;
- Investigate the facts with the complainant, the person about whom the complaint has been made and any witnesses;
- Look for supporting evidence;
- Ask the complainant about his preferred outcome (he may not want to make a formal complaint, but be satisfied with an apology).

Informal Approaches

In some cases it may be possible to put matters right informally. Sometimes people are not aware that their behaviour is unwelcome and an informal discussion can lead to greater understanding and an agreement that the behaviour will stop. It may be that the individual will choose to do this himself, or he may need support from Human Resources, a manager or another staff member.

Disciplinary Procedures

Where an informal resolution is not possible, you may decide that the matter is a disciplinary issue which needs to be dealt with formally at the appropriate level of the organisation's disciplinary procedure. As with any disciplinary problem it is important to follow a fair procedure. In the case of a complaint of bullying or harassment there must be fairness to both the complainant and the person accused.

In cases which appear to involve serious misconduct, and there is reason to separate the parties, you may need to consider a short period of suspension of the alleged bully/harasser while the case is being investigated. This should be with pay. A suspension without pay, or any long suspension with pay, should be exceptional as these in themselves may amount to disciplinary penalties. Don't transfer the person making the complaint unless he asks for such a move.

There may be cases where somebody makes an unfounded allegation of bullying and/or harassment for malicious reasons. These cases should also be investigated and dealt with fairly and objectively under the disciplinary procedure.

Conclusions

Any action taken will be determined by the facts of the case and must be reasonable in the circumstances. In some cases a disciplinary penalty is inappropriate and counselling or training is preferable. Where a disciplinary penalty is imposed, all the circumstances should be considered including:

- ❑ The employee's disciplinary and general record;
- ❑ Whether the procedure points to a particular penalty, action taken in previous cases;
- ❑ Any explanations and circumstances to be considered and the reasonableness of the penalty.

Whenever a case of bullying or harassment arises, you should take the opportunity to examine policies, procedures and working methods to see if they can be improved and reiterate acceptable standards of behaviour to staff.

Section 8   Special Cases

Employees To Whom The Full Procedure Is Not Immediately Available

It may be sensible to arrange time off with pay so that employees who are in isolated locations or on shifts can attend a disciplinary hearing on the main site in normal working hours. Alternatively, if a number of witnesses need to attend it may be better to hold the disciplinary hearing on the nightshift or at the particular location.

Trade Union Officials

Normal disciplinary standards apply to their conduct as employees. However no action beyond first stage disciplinary procedures should apply to their conduct without discussing the issues with a full time official.

Criminal Acts At Work

The normal disciplinary procedures outlined in this book still apply and you should follow them.

Criminal Acts Or Misbehaviour Outside The Workplace

ACAS recommend that a criminal offence outside employment should not automatically be treated as grounds for dismissal. The main consideration is whether the offence makes the employee committing it unsuitable for the job for which he's employed or unacceptable to other employees. So for example, where a team leader who worked for a big department store was convicted of shop lifting in another shop, it was fair to dismiss her because the offence was relevant to her position.

Section 9   Grievances

A grievance is a ground of complaint raised with the employer by an employee against another employee or against the employer himself.

What do you do when an employee comes to you with a problem? In other words, if he has cause for complaint regarding his duties, conditions of employment, working conditions or procedures, how do you deal with the situation?

Keep disciplinary and grievance procedures quite separate, although there may be occasions when a grievance could result in disciplinary action (for instance a complaint about bullying or harassment might lead to formal disciplinary action against the alleged bully/harasser). Grievances may also be raised against line managers, and if they are the first stage in the procedure then you need to consider how to deal with the issue. In these circumstances the matter is usually referred to a senior manager who can decide who should best hear the grievance.

Failure to respond to a grievance appropriately can result in a constructive dismissal claim. It is an employee's right to air a genuine grievance. Every company employing staff, however small the business, must have a process by which an employee can formally raise a grievance to his employer's attention. Raising a grievance does not automatically entitle staff to have their own way, but it does require that an issue is properly examined and considered by the employer.

Individual grievances should be settled as near to the point of origin of the grievance as possible. This means that in the first instance the immediate supervisor should deal with it. Whenever a grievance goes beyond that stage, the appropriate supervisor should continue to be involved in the subsequent decision-making. If the supervisor's initial response is to be altered at a later stage, he should be asked his opinion and informed of the reasoning behind the amended action.

Many grievances can be dealt with informally by an immediate line manager. Encouraging members of staff to raise their concerns in this way often leads to a quick solution.

Make it clear that grievance proceedings and records will be kept in confidence. Staff going through the formal grievance procedure have the right to be accompanied by a union representative or workplace colleague at meetings. Once agreed, make sure that your employees have easy access to a copy of the procedure and that you explain the process to new members of staff, as part of their induction. Remember to make special arrangements for employees whose first language is not English, those who have a visual or hearing impairment or other disability.

The aim of your procedure should be to settle the grievance in the shortest possible time. There shouldn't be any unreasonable delays in arranging meetings at each stage of the process and employees shouldn't be left in a state of suspense, not knowing whether any action is being taken or when they will be told of the decision.

Monitor grievances, both in terms of issues raised and outcomes agreed. Issues that constantly give rise to grievances may highlight a specific problem. It can also be a useful way of monitoring employee morale.

Grievance Meeting

The grievance interview requires the skills of any interview situation. Consider the following points when training your supervisors in handling the company's grievance procedure:

- Provide an appropriate physical environment free from interruptions;
- Listen to, and hear, what the employee is saying;
- Ask appropriate questions in a non-threatening way;
- Analyse the facts and take a decision;
- Develop an ability to say 'no' firmly, without rancour, but with a clear explanation.

Formal Grievance Hearing

If informal discussions are not successful, try the following process:

- The employee puts the complaint formally to the line manager, preferably in writing. If the grievance is against the line manager, it should be raised with a more senior manager;
- The manager invites the employee to a hearing to discuss the grievance and informs the employee that he has the right to be accompanied;
- At the hearing the employee puts his views to the manager;
- The manager responds to the grievance in writing by the deadline given in your company's procedure. You might, for example, expect managers to respond within five working days of the hearing. If the deadline cannot be met, the manager should explain the reasons to the employee and say when a response can be expected;
- If dissatisfied, the employee raises the matter with a senior manager named in the procedure. Depending on the company, this might be a director, the managing director or chief executive. The same principles of holding a formal meeting and providing a response by an agreed deadline apply;
- It is a good idea to identify a third party to whom an employee can take his grievance if it concerns harassment or bullying and he feels he cannot take it to his line manager.

Checklist Grievance Procedure

Your grievance procedure should be a formal written document. There is no generic procedure that is applicable to all organisations, but you should bear the following in mind when developing a grievance procedure:

- ☐ Preamble: The majority of grievance procedures begin with a statement of why a formal procedure is necessary.
- ☐ Coverage: The procedure should describe the issues to be included and what should be excluded, for example, safety.
- ☐ Stages: Grievance procedures should set out the stages through which a grievance is heard within the organisational hierarchy. This recognises the authority and responsibility of the parties at the different levels within the company and allows for a structured approach to the situation. The number of stages in your procedure is, to some extent, determined by the structure of your organisation. In practical terms, three to four stages are the most appropriate. Any more than this can lead to a procedure that is unwieldy, slow and potentially confusing.
- ☐ Investigation: At each stage of the procedure the reviewer is likely to conduct an information search of policies, procedures, practices, collective agreements, operating instructions, interviews, etc. This involves defining the issue, ascertaining the facts and collecting any relevant records. If the case goes to a third-party hearing, then preparing arguments, selecting a spokesperson and testing the strength of the case have to be considered.
- ☐ Levels: There are usually three levels for hearing grievances - supervisors, departmental managers and senior managers, but this is not mandatory.
- ☐ Outcome: The outcome of the grievance must be notified to your employee in writing, with a statement of his right to take the grievance to the next stage of the procedure if he is dissatisfied with the reviewer's decision.

Appendix 1 Sample Capability Procedure

1. Purpose

This procedure is designed to deal with those cases where the employee is lacking in some area of knowledge, skill or ability, resulting in a failure to be able to carry out the required duties to an acceptable standard. It is to be used where there is a genuine lack of capability, rather than a deliberate failure on the part of the employee to perform to the standards of which he is capable (for which use of the disciplinary procedure is appropriate). A genuine lack of capability may have been present for some time or may have come about more recently because of, for example, changing job content or personal factors affecting the individual's performance.

The procedure seeks to:

i.   Assist the employee to improve his performance, wherever possible, where such deficiencies exist.

ii.   Provide a firm but fair and consistent means of dealing with capability problems without employing the disciplinary procedure.

iii.   Provide a means of solving capability problems where improvement in the current job is not possible.

2. Application

The procedure applies to all the Company's employees other than the Chief Executive.

3. Informal Assistance

Nothing in this procedure is intended to prevent the normal process of supervision control whereby line managers allocate work, monitor performance, draw attention to errors and poor quality and highlight work done well. This may include informal assistance in achieving improvement. Such methods are not part of the formal performance management procedure and therefore formal interviews and representation are not appropriate to this everyday process. Line managers should maintain personal notes of difficulties encountered, assistance given and any remedial actions taken for future reference in case formal action is needed; the employee is entitled to have a copy of such notes.

4. Representation

At all stages of the formal procedure an employee is entitled to have a representative present, who may be a fellow employee or trade union representative. It will be made clear in advance to the employee (and to the representative, if the employee exercises this option) that the performance management rather than the disciplinary procedure is being used.

If at any stage a line manager has reason to believe that the non-capability is due to poor conduct or lack of effort on the part of the employee, he will stop the process and may set up a disciplinary interview at a later date in accordance with that procedure. He will inform the employee clearly of the change of procedure and repeat that there is a right to representation if this has not previously been taken up.

5. The Formal Procedure

Stage 1 – Formal Counselling

Where an employee is failing to perform to an acceptable standard, despite having been given informal guidance and assistance, a formal counselling session (giving at least 24 hours notice) will be arranged with him by his line manager. During this counselling the employee will be told clearly of the deficiencies which have been identified and precisely of the improvement in work standard which is required (with the possible consequences of not doing so). There must be an opportunity for the employee to answer these points and to explain any difficulties which he may be having, and a discussion on the ways and means by which the desired improvement may be achieved. Appropriate possibilities would include:

i.   Training, either external or internal;
ii.   Working under closer supervision from a line manager, or a work colleague who is competent and experienced in the work for an agreed specified period;
iii. Agreed changes in duties, either permanently or for a trial period.

The conclusions from this counselling session will be formally recorded in writing, with a copy given to the employee.

A reasonable timescale for improvement will be set (the length to be determined by individual circumstances but normally not longer than two months), with monitoring during that period and a review meeting at the end of it. If the desired improvement has been achieved, this will be recorded and the employee will be given a copy of the file note.

Stage 2 – Formal Warning

If the desired improvement has not been achieved, the employee will be clearly told of the continued deficiencies by his line manager at the review meeting. The remedial measures previously agreed will also be reviewed and there will be discussion on whether they should continue or whether additional measures might be helpful. The employee will again be afforded the right to answer the points made and explain his problems.

It may be felt appropriate at this stage to discuss whether a permanent redeployment would be possible and if so, an agreeable option for the employee. This may be particularly appropriate for an employee who has not been able to cope with a promotion but was satisfactory in the previous job. If this is an agreed possibility the employee's director will be notified and the further steps required to implement this solution will be under his control. In cases where there is redeployment to a post on a lower grade there will be no salary protection.

The review meeting will be followed by a formal letter to the employee setting out the continued deficiencies, the expected improvement, the timescale for achieving it, the further help which will be given, any agreed changes to the employment contract and that a failure to achieve the improvement within the timescale will necessitate a consideration of whether employment should be terminated. It therefore acts as a final warning letter and the employee's director will be formally notified in writing to ensure he is aware of the action taken. It will also set out the employee's right of appeal, including to whom it should be made and the time limit for doing so.

A reasonable timescale for improvements will be set (again normally not longer than two months), with monitoring during that period and a review meeting at the end of it. If the desired improvement has been achieved, this will be recorded and the employee will be given a copy of the file note.

Stage 3 – Final Resolution

If the desired improvement has still not been achieved, the review meeting must be held by the employee's director, and the employee will again be clearly told of the continued deficiencies and offered the opportunity to answer any points made. The director will then make a decision as to whether there is any likelihood of the employee's performance achieving an acceptable level by extending the assistance offered and timescale allowed under the previous stage.

If the decision is that performance will not become acceptable in the current post, a further consideration of whether permanent redeployment (at the same or lower pay level) is possible, and of whether the alternative job is likely to be performed acceptably by the employee, will be made. If no suitable alternative employment is available, or the employee refuses the redeployment, termination of employment will take place, with notice or pay in lieu of notice being given.

The fact of and reasons for this termination, the last date of employment, any necessary administrative or financial arrangements, and to whom, and within what time limit, any appeal should be made, will immediately be confirmed to the employee in writing.

6. Appeals

An appeal right exists at stages two and three of the formal procedure. There will not be a delay in implementing management decisions pending the appeal, but they may be subsequently reversed as a result of the appeal hearing.

Appeals must be lodged within seven working days of receipt of either a warning or termination of employment letter, and the appeal hearing must take place within the next 15 working days (unless the parties agree to a delay). The employee has the same right of representation at an appeal as during the above formal stages.

Appeals against decisions of line managers will be heard by the departmental director, those against decisions of a director by the Chief Executive. Appeals against decisions of the Chief Executive will be heard by another director.

The procedure at appeal hearings will be the same as for formal grievance hearings, except that the management case will be heard first and the employee's second.

7. Capability of Managers and Directors

The principles and procedures in the preceding paragraphs apply to managers and directors as much as to other employees, but the stages in their cases will need to be undertaken at different levels. For managers, all stages within the procedure will be undertaken by their director, with appeals being heard by the Chief Executive. The Chief Executive will handle all capability issues in relation to directors, with appeals to the Chairman of the Board.

Appendix 2 Sample Absence Management Procedure

1. Introduction

As an employer the Company has an obvious wish to ensure regular attendance at work on the part of its employees. In addition, as a good employer, it wishes to take an interest in the health and welfare of the people whom it employs. It also seeks to ensure that undue pressure is minimized for those people whose attendance record is good and whose workload is increased as a result of staff sickness. This personnel procedure is designed to provide a framework within which the Company can achieve these important objectives.

The procedure sets out some formal steps to provide such a framework, but this does not prevent managers from carrying out a supportive welfare role in informally meeting staff with health difficulties and problems and assisting them in any way which may be appropriate.

Throughout this procedure all information concerning an employee's health will be treated in the strictest confidence.

As part of a line manager's role, home visits to employees on long term sickness absence or in other circumstances where the line manager thinks it appropriate are positively encouraged.

2. Short Term Sickness

Short-term absences may be defined as those which last for less than eight calendar days (including weekends and bank holidays) and are therefore certified by the individual rather than by a medical practitioner. In considering employees' records of absence of this nature, line managers will take into account the pattern as well as the total amount of sickness absence.

First Stage

If a line manager feels that there is an unusually high level of sickness absence e.g. more than ten days within a twelve month period, he should meet the employee in the context of a welfare discussion. The first assumption should be that the employee has been absent for genuine medical reasons, unless there is specific evidence to the contrary. This should be made clear to the employee, so that there are no grounds for believing that an attempt to discipline him concerning absences is being made at this stage. The employee should be encouraged to talk about his reasons for absence, what medical or other help is being provided to him at present and whether he would like the Company's assistance in any way to try to resolve the problems.

Second Stage

Where short-term absences continue to take place despite the above counselling and offers of assistance, the line manager should see the employee again. As before, the interview should normally be held in the context of a counselling and welfare discussion, but on this occasion, the desirability of a referral for independent medical advice should be discussed. If both the Company and the employee agree that this would be helpful in identifying and remedying the problem, arrangements should be made by the line manager for this to happen, with any necessary fees paid for by the Company. Following the interview, the line manager should write to the employee confirming the main points covered and any assistance which has been offered, and indicating that the employee's record will continue to be kept under review.

Third Stage

If there is still no improvement within the next two or three months (or if absences start to recur after that period) the line manager should see the employee again. At this stage, if it has not been done before, arrangements must be made for independent medical advice to be obtained, on the same terms as stage two. Where that advice does not identify causal medical factors and there are no other mitigating factors, a letter should be sent to the employee making it clear that his attendance record is not acceptable and that an immediate and sustained improvement must be made if future employment is not to be jeopardised.

It may be that the employee refuses to undergo a medical examination. He should be assured of his right to a copy of the report which is obtained, but if there is still a refusal the employee cannot be forced to comply. However, subsequent decisions as to appropriate actions, including termination of employment, are not prevented from being made because of such a refusal. It is for the employer to make a reasonable judgement on all the facts which may be available, which should include medical evidence if possible, but which may also be made in its absence if the employee objects without reason.

Consideration Of Termination of Employment

If after a further short period (the length of which will be determined by circumstances) there is still no improvement, termination of employment will have to be considered. At this stage it becomes important to decide whether the absence is genuinely for ill-health or if it is not for legitimate health reasons.

If the sickness absence is genuine the context of termination is an inability of the employee to properly discharge his duties. In this case consideration should be given to possibilities such as redeployment to an easier job, reductions in hours or use of appropriate adaptations, if these would present an acceptable solution which may replace a decision to terminate. His director should discuss the problem frankly and fully with him and then notify him of the decision made in the light of that discussion. A right of appeal to the Chief Executive should be given.

If it is considered that the absence is not for genuine health reasons the matter should be considered as misconduct and the disciplinary procedure invoked. Deliberate non-attendance at work may be regarded as gross misconduct, depending on the circumstances and therefore the employee should be informed that the result of a disciplinary hearing may be dismissal.

Representation

At all stages of this procedure, employees will be afforded the right to have a trade union representative or work colleague present.

3. Long Term Sickness

The circumstances which give rise to absence of this type are usually quite different to those causing short-term absence. These will almost always be cases where an employee has a substantial and often on-going illness, or has been subject to some form of major injury. Because absence is long-term it will be supported by a doctor's or hospital medical certificates. The approach set out above for dealing with short-term absences is unsuitable for these circumstances. Instead decisions are required to be taken in the light of the medical evidence and on the basis of balancing the needs of the Company and the capabilities of the employee.

Regard must also be had to the Disability Discrimination Act 1995 (DDA) which requires employers to provide reasonable assistance, resources and support to employees with a long-term physical or mental impairment, whether that came about before or since employment was taken up. This is, therefore, an issue requiring a welfare approach and it should never be dealt with as a disciplinary matter.

Any employee who has been absent on certified sick leave for more than a month should by then have had contact with his line manager by telephone and/ or by visits to ascertain his progress and to determine whether there is any practical assistance which the Company could give. This should be done in the context of genuine welfare assistance and not in any way as to intrude into the employee's privacy or harass the employee as to when he will be coming back

Return to Work

When an employee who has been long-term sick returns to work, his line manager should arrange to see him at the earliest opportunity to provide a welcome, ensure that there is fitness for work (some people do come back too soon because they are concerned about their jobs or because they go through the time limits for reduction in pay) and to update him on the current work in the department. Any problems of a major nature e.g. not really fit for work, should be referred to a director.

Under the DDA there must be an assessment of the support and needs required for the employee to attend work. This includes looking at issues such as reduced hours for a period of rehabilitation (or longer), reasonable adjustments to the workplace and/ or working conditions, reasonable adaptations or modifications to the premises and equipment and possible reallocation of duties.

Reasonable time off to attend medical appointments must also be given.

Incomplete Recovery

If the employee is unlikely to recover sufficiently to enable a return to his full previous duties, the possibility of finding alternatives or a reduced level of work must be considered. There is no obligation to create an unnecessary job to meet the employee's needs, but all reasonable steps should be taken to identify a job which the employee is able to do – where appropriate with the benefit of training and again by making suitable adaptations to the workplace and/ or equipment.

A further possibility, if the employee agrees, is practical assistance (time off, references etc) in the finding of less onerous or more suitable employment outside the Company.

No Prospect of Recovery

In cases where it becomes clear from all the evidence and after proper assessment under the DDA, that it is really not practicable for the employee to return either to his previous job or to other employment within the Company, termination on grounds of ill-health needs to be considered. It must be considered in consultation with the employee and it is not in any sense a disciplinary matter.

The ultimate decision should be taken by the employee's director and only after the receipt of medical reports which support the view that there will not be fitness for work in the foreseeable future and normally not until at least six months has occurred. In considering timescales, the nature of the position held by the employee, the importance of replacing him and the feasibility of providing interim cover are valid factors, so an earlier decision may in some cases be appropriate.

If termination is felt to be necessary, the employee must be seen by his director and advised beforehand that he has a right to be accompanied by a fellow employee or trade union representative. Sufficient time should be allowed for the employee to arrange for this accompaniment and this may be of the order of ten days to two weeks. The employee should be informed of the medical conclusions, asked for his views, consulted regarding the feasibility of alternative employment and presented with the realities of the situation. It should also be ascertained that the employee is fully aware of any entitlement to State benefits.

There may be agreement that termination is the only option or that another option should be pursued. However, it may also be necessary to terminate without the employee's agreement and the employee must be advised of a right of appeal to the Chief Executive in this case.

Terminal Illness

In cases where it is clear that illness is leading to death in the near future, it would be inappropriate to embark on formal procedures and welfare assistance to the employee and his family should be provided as far as possible.

Appendix 3 Sample Disciplinary Procedures and Rules

1. Purpose and Scope

The Company's aim is to encourage improvement in individual conduct. This procedure sets out the action which will be taken when disciplinary rules are breached.

In the employee's first year of employment, the Short Service Disciplinary Procedure applies. The Company reserves the right in its absolute discretion to reduce the number of formal warnings to one where the employee is in the first year of service. If the employee's performance or conduct does not meet the standards required by the Company at the due review date, the next stage will be dismissal. All other principles of the Company's disciplinary procedure apply.

1 Principles

The procedure is designed to deal consistently with disciplinary issues. No disciplinary action will be taken until the matter has been fully investigated.
At every stage employees will have the opportunity to state their case and be accompanied by a fellow employee or trade union representative if they wish.

An employee has the right to appeal against any disciplinary penalty.

Managers are authorised to deal with any disciplinary matter to Stage 3. Only the Managing Director may authorise a dismissal.

2. The Procedure

Informal Discussions/ Counselling

Other than in a matter of serious misconduct, where an employee's standard of conduct or performance etc is considered lacking, or a breach of conduct is believed to have occurred, his manager will normally draw the matter to his attention in a private and informal way.

In most cases this informal discussion should resolve any difficulties identified. If the employee fails to improve, or sustain improvement, the formal procedure will commence.

Notification

If conduct or performance fails to meet acceptable standards, the individual will be given 72 hours notice in writing of a disciplinary meeting in the form of a letter in which he will be advised of the details of the alleged breach of discipline. This time can be reduced by mutual agreement.

The letter will enclose supporting documents e.g. copies of paperwork, details of performance, etc as appropriate. The letter will contain a reminder that all staff have the right to be accompanied by a fellow worker or a trade union representative.

The Hearing

A manager, who may be accompanied by another manager or the Company's human resources advisor, will conduct the disciplinary hearing. Throughout the hearing, minutes will be taken for the record. At the hearing the following will occur:

a) The employee will be advised of his rights.
b) The employee will be advised of all known facts relevant to the case.
c) The employee will be given every opportunity to put forward his case and views. His companion will be invited to make representations on his behalf.
There will be an adjournment to consider the facts.
d) At the end of the hearing, the employee will be advised of the decision of the manager.
e) If a disciplinary penalty is awarded, the manager will advise the employee of his right of appeal.

Stage 1 - Oral Warning

If conduct or performance is unsatisfactory, the employee will be given an oral warning which will be recorded. The warning will be disregarded after six months satisfactory service.

Repetition of this or any other matter of misconduct during the life of the warning will result in an escalation to the next stage of the disciplinary process.

This applies at every level of the disciplinary procedure.

Stage 2 - Written Warning

If the offence is serious or if there is no improvement in standards or if a further offence occurs, a written warning will be given. This will include a reason for the warning and a note that, if there is no improvement a final written warning will be given. The written warning will remain live for twelve months. If there is no repetition or other offence, it will be disregarded after that time.

Stage 3 - Final Written Warning

If conduct or performance is still unsatisfactory, a final written warning will be given making it clear that any recurrence of the offence or other serious misconduct will result in dismissal. The final written warning will remain live for twelve months. If there is no repetition or other offence, it will be disregarded after that time.

Stage 4 - Dismissal

If there is no satisfactory improvement or if further serious misconduct occurs, the employee will be dismissed.

Gross Misconduct

If, after investigation, it is confirmed that an employee has committed an offence of the following nature (the list is not exhaustive), the normal consequences will be summary dismissal (dismissal without notice):

Theft
Damage to company property
Fraud
Incapacity for work due to being under the influence of alcohol or illegal drugs
Physical assault
Gross insubordination.
Failure to comply with relevant statutory or regulatory requirements
Violent, abusive or intimidating conduct
Sexual, racial or other harassment
Unauthorised use or disclosure of confidential information
Reckless or serious misuse of a Company vehicle
Rudeness to customers
Accepting a gift which could be construed as a bribe
Breach of health and safety rules which endanger the health and safety of others in the opinion of the Company.
Refusing to allow a search to be carried out in accordance with Company rules
Failure to disclose correct information on your application form
Conviction for any serious criminal offence while an employee of the Company
Downloading of or sending of inappropriate material in contravention of the Company's email and internet policy
Behaviour whether inside or outside work which may bring the Company into disrepute

Suspension

Where there is an allegation of gross misconduct the Company reserves the right to suspend an employee on full pay during a disciplinary investigation. During the period of suspension the employee will be paid the normal hourly rate. Any decision to dismiss will be taken by the Company only after a full investigation and disciplinary hearing.

The suspension will be for as short a time as is reasonably possible in the circumstances. This will not normally exceed five working days. The employee must remain available to answer the Company's questions at all times during a period of suspension.

Stage 5 - Appeals

An employee who wishes to appeal against any disciplinary decision must do so to [name] or an independent third party nominated by the Company within five working days. The named person will hear the appeal and decide the case as impartially as possible.

Where new evidence comes to light during the appeal which was not available at the original hearing, the person hearing the appeal will remit the matter back to the original disciplining manager.

Hearing in the Absence of an Employee

While the Company will make every effort to ensure that an employee is able to attend a disciplinary hearing, the Company reserves the right to hear a case in his absence if, after several attempts to reschedule, he has failed to attend the hearing.

Levels of Disciplinary Action

There are several potential levels, these are:

- ❑ Oral Warning
- ❑ Written Warning
- ❑ Final Written Warning
- ❑ Dismissal/Demotion
- ❑ Summary Dismissal

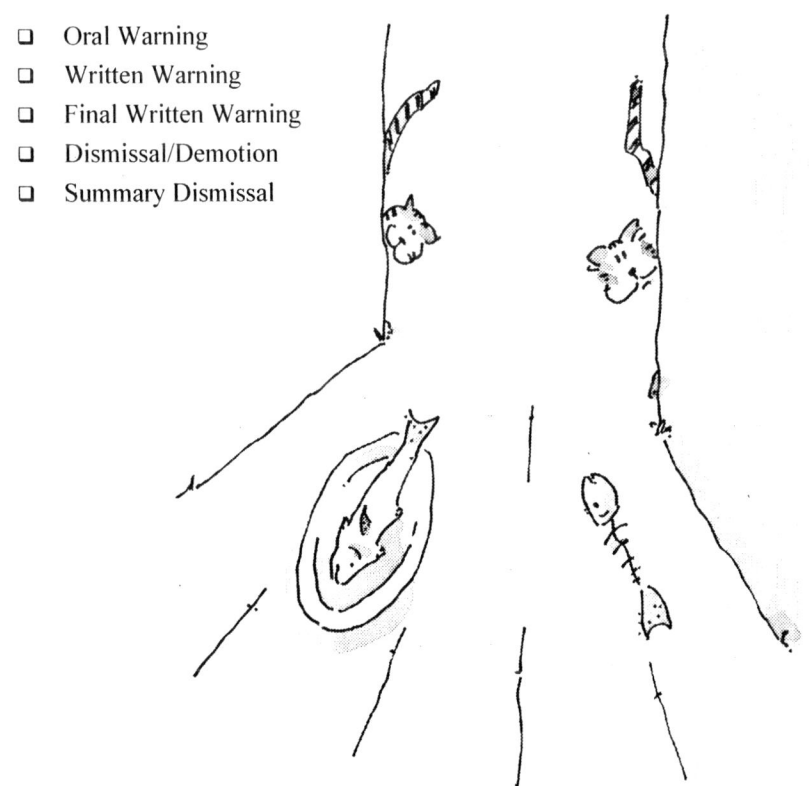

Useful Contacts

ACAS
Tel: 08457 474747   www.acas.org.uk

Criminal Records Agency
Tel: 0870 9090 811   www.crb.gov.uk

Commission for Racial Equality
Tel 020 7939 0000   www.cre.gov.uk

Disability Rights Commission
Tel 08457 622 633   www.drc.org.uk

DTI
Tel: 020 7215 5000   www.dti.gov.uk

Equal Opportunities Commission
Tel 08456 015 901   www.eoc.org.uk

Home Office
Tel: 0870 000 1585   www.homeoffice.gov.uk

Immigration and Nationality Directorate
Tel: 0870 606 7766   www.ind.homeoffice.gov.uk

Index

By the same author

If you found this book helpful, you might like to know about *"101 Tips For Employers"*. Soaring levels of awards and constantly changing legislation make the area of employment law the daily equivalent of walking a tightrope for a busy company. These include, but are not limited to unfair dismissal, sex, race, disability discrimination and so on. Lack of knowledge can land employers in an employment tribunal, often on the losing side. *101 Tips* is a useful and clear reference for busy employers.

What the users say:

"Crisp, concise and clear, an excellent resource for busy managers." *Bill Ashworth, Head of IT, Countrywide Surveyors*

"With the amount of employment legislation ever increasing, this book represents a handy, user friendly tool to help and guide the busy manager through what can be a minefield of information and interpretation when trying to run a business on a day to day basis. It does not try to provide an exhaustive account of the law, but rather to highlight and advise on the most significant areas which are likely to cause problems and to point out the trends in the development of the law. An invaluable aid for anyone involved in managing people." *Andrea Hughes, HR Manager, Glenair UK Ltd*

"I think it is excellent. Every employer should have one. It is easy to digest and full of good basic information." *Judith de Jong, Managing Director, JKL (Training & Consultancy) Ltd*

"Working in the financial services sector, where the day to day pressures are to focus on the client, profit margins and deadlines, it is often easy to forget about one of the most valuable assets of the organisation, the employees and what their rights are. The 101 Tips for Employers is an incredibly useful tool to remind managers of the importance of making time to focus on the treatment of their employees. The area of employment law is a minefield, but a little bit of knowledge now can go a long way to preventing a more serious problem in the future.' *Clare Ratnavira, IT Director, ING Bank NV*

"101 Tips has been of benefit to us twofold. I have been able to refer to it for my own staffing issues in my own business (international recruitment) as well as being able to have a broader, more informed knowledge of some of the issues faced by my clients to whom I have been able to recommend it.

An excellent source of reference, it is well laid out, highly informative and contains all the main question topics in an easily digestible format." *Julie Holmwood, Managing Director, Eton Mai*

Printed in the United Kingdom
by Lightning Source UK Ltd.
111257UKS00001B/107